The Parable of the Four Stones:
Finding Your Path of Purpose

Jeff M. Brewer

Copyright © 2008 by Jeff M. Brewer

The Parable of the Four Stones
Finding Your Path of Purpose
by Jeff M. Brewer

Printed in the United States of America

ISBN 978-1-60647-617-8

All rights reserved solely by the author. The author guarantees all contents are original and do not infringe upon the legal rights of any other person or work. No part of this book may be reproduced in any form without the permission of the author. The views expressed in this book are not necessarily those of the publisher.

Bible quotations are taken from the New Living Translation version of the Bible. Copyright © 2005 by Tyndale House Publishers, Inc.

www.xulonpress.com

Editor

James Ratcliff

A 1974 graduate of George Washington University, Jim is a missionary and a writer. Before finding his path of purpose, he hiked in the Himalayas, looked into the eyeball of a sleeping shark in the Mexican Caribbean, and broke his toe in Greece when he stubbed it on a stone. His personal vision is to help people discover God's path without breaking their toes on the stones.

Dedication

I dedicate this book to all people; for we are a people of destiny, uniquely designed for a higher purpose than ourselves. I dedicate this book to those who struggle to find their path of purpose and those walking on their path of purpose. May we all find our path and stay the course.

Acknowledgements

I am inspired by my wife, Kim, who has entrusted me with her love, her friendship and her dedication for over 34 years. She has been the biggest blessing in my life and I honor her. A day does not go by she doesn't encourage me and challenge me to grow. I thank God every day for her! I love you honey!

I am in constant thankfulness for my children Jessica and Martin, who have spent the past 30 years teaching me how to be a good father and loving me in spite of myself. A father could not ask for better children. I am so proud of who they are and their commitment to Jesus Christ.

I thank God for my children's spouses, Jeremy and Jennifer, who are a true God-send and answer to years of prayer. Jeremy is my friend, my golf and fishing partner, a great Dad to my grandchildren and a Godly husband for my daughter. Jennifer is a second daughter to me; she loves my son and is a Godly wife to him.

My life has been enriched beyond measure by Lindy, Laney and Landon, my three grandchildren. Their wisdom, their energy, their personalities make life fun and interesting.

I love and honor my Pastor, Leadership Strategist, Keith Craft. He challenges me to live a life of Transformation; Loving, Learning and Leading. I thank you Pastor for being a disciplined, Godly man, my mentor and my friend.

The "Mighty Men" – you know who you are; you know what you bring and you know I love all you guys! And our leader, Scott Unclebach, you are an unselfish friend and I love and appreciate you immensely. Thank you for challenging me to be my best.

Dr. Joe Fawcett, my health and wellness coach, I honor you. Thank you for allowing me to record our conversation and thanks for being a friend closer than a brother. To LouAnn Fawcett, you are a Godly-woman, a close friend of our family and an example for all women. Thank you for being in our lives. Jonathan Fawcett, your talent amazes me. It is refreshing to see a bright young man using his talents for God.

My friends Phillip and Melissa Moss, who live their lives and walk out their dreams transparently in front of all people. I appreciate your prayers, your encouragement and the opportunity to go through life with you.

My newest friend, my editor, Jim Ratcliff, who never ceases to amaze, challenge and bless me while bringing it all together. Jim, you are a God-send!

I thank my family for always loving me, guiding me and believing in me: my parents Robert J and Dorothy Brewer (deceased and not forgotten), my wife's parents Herman and Becky Bentley (deceased and not forgotten), my sister Bobbie and husband Chris Cooley, Marc and Kyleen Bentley, John

Bentley, Ben and Louise Spain, and all my Aunts, Uncles and Cousins. I am blessed to be in such a family as this.

These men and women have positively impacted my life and I thank them for their love, direction and helping me be a better man:
- Pastor Walter Hallam, Pastor – Abundant Life Christian Center
- Pastor Al Jandl, Pastor – Living Stones Church
- Mark Panzer, my CPA and my friend
- Dr. Kishore Nadkarni, my former supervisor at Exxon R&D; a great man
- Dick Flynn, my former supervisor at Dionex
- Coach Doug McGown, one of the best volleyball coaches on earth
- My Uncle Walter Brewer (deceased but not forgotten), like a second dad!
- Hazel Clement (deceased but not forgotten), my supervisor at Exxon in the early days
- Stan Taylor, our youth Pastor at Pasadena First Church of the Nazarene
- Ray Witt, my choir director in High School
- Tommy Oakes (deceased but not forgotten), a loyal friend who taught me the purpose of tithing and a great musician.
- Dr. Barry Streusand, President – Applied Analytical Inc. in Round Rock, TX. He is a good friend and golf partner.
- Adrian Deteindre, Jan Geil, Dr. Helwig Schafer, Dr. Markus Laeubli, Dr. Kai Veihweger, some of my friends from Switzlerand.
- William E. (Bill) Fitch, my former VP, golf partner and friend
- Derrick Rowe, my former VP, right hand man, and a great fisherman

- Christina Pauley, my former Administrative Assistant. Loyal, trustworthy and a joy to around. Kim and I honor you!

Any time I undertake an acknowledgement I forget someone important. Please know it is an oversight on my part, forgive me and know you have impacted my life and I honor you.

CONTENTS

Introduction xv

The Parable of the Four Stones 19

1 What We Ought to Be 55

2 The Path of Default 73

3 The Path of Choice 83

4 Vision 97

5 Plan 109

6 Balance 121

7 Action 131

8 Cocoon Season 141

9 On This Rock 151

INTRODUCTION

Satisfaction Guaranteed

What would life be like if satisfaction was guaranteed? Not laundry detergent or some other household product, but life itself. Hard to imagine, isn't it?

I wrote this book to give ordinary people the tools they need to live more fulfilling lives. When people apply these tools to their daily lives, they begin to experience a degree of satisfaction they've never known before. As you read this book, you'll learn how to approach every challenge and every obstacle in your life as if you were guaranteed of success. Get ready for a life-changing experience.

What will it take to attain satisfaction in your life? The answer isn't as complicated as most people think. It just takes a proven system and a clear strategy for implementing that system. Generation after generation, ordinary men and women in all walks of life and all cultures have discovered that God's system of Biblical success works.

If the solution is so attainable, why haven't most people reached it already? In many cases, they don't have an easy-to-understand and easy-to-use implementation system. *The Parable of the Four Stones: Finding Your Path of Purpose* explains in clear language how to put God's system of Biblical success to work in your life.

My life isn't always smooth sailing; I continually evaluate my choices in an effort to eliminate or minimize obstacles. When I face an obstacle, I don't face it alone. I have chosen a Lord and Savior, Jesus Christ, who guides me through obstacles and carries me over the slippery stones if I let him. When I face obstacles on my own, I sometimes have to back up and start over. I achieve more with Christ in my life than without him.

'For We Have the Mind of Christ'

Almost 2,000 years ago, the apostle Paul wrote, "But we understand these things, for we have the mind of Christ" (1 Corinthians 2:16). The first time I heard that in church, it sounded impossible.

I thought to myself, *how can ordinary people—people like me—have the mind of the person that had the mind of God?*

When I heard that verse in church the first time, I admired the speaker's noble intentions, but I questioned his sanity. I didn't think it was a literal possibility in the "real world." To my untransformed mind, the Bible was full of noble, but impossible, ideas.

I wrote this book to help you understand that what the Bible says is true. Biologically and spiritually speaking, we have the mind of Christ. Think about it. The man that lived 2,000 years ago as Jesus of Nazareth had the brain of an ordinary human being. Biologically speaking, every person in the world has the mind of Christ. And spiritually speaking, God will give us a new mind—one that's more like the mind of Christ than like the one we used to have—if we let him.

The Spirit of God transforms ordinary people—people like you and me—into people that are more like Christ than like the people they used to be. The transformation of ordinary human beings is not only a literal possibility, but a never-ending fact of life in the "real world." It's happening somewhere, to somebody, at every hour, minute, and second of the day. It's a process that's available to people in all time zones and cultures.

I have discovered in my own life what people have known for the last two millennia: that it's possible to stop living by default and to start living by design; it's possible to make the right choices; it's possible to follow a path of God's best for your life; it's possible to make the choices Christ would make if he were in your shoes.

How do I know these things? I know them because God has given me a new mind by changing the way I think. And though these things were never lost, I have "discovered" them in the New Testament stories of men and women that were transformed into people who resembled Jesus more than they resembled their former selves.

The book you're about to read is no ordinary book. It comes with a lifetime guarantee. Unlike many one-time offers and special promotions, it isn't void in Ohio or anywhere else. Everyone is eligible. Anyone can participate.

Here's the deal: Use *The Four Stones* to find your path of purpose. If you do, you'll be satisfied the rest of your life. I guarantee it.

To get started, simply accept the "Terms & Conditions":
1. Applying *The Four Stones* in your life DOES NOT lead to problem-free living. (The Bible is clear on this point.)
2. Applying *The Four Stones* in your life DOES empower you to overcome obstacles that keep you from living a more satisfying life.
3. For the purposes of this agreement, "SATISFACTION" is defined not as a state of life in which problems no longer exist, but as a state of mind that exists when

people have the power to overcome obstacles and rise above problems.

Here's the deal:
1. Read this book and implement *The Four Stones* in your life.
2. Get on and stay on God's path for your life.
3. If you decide, after carrying out the steps above, that this book hasn't made a positive difference in your life, I'll give you your money back.

As readers, we don't really want our money back. We want a way to overcome obstacles that keep us from living fulfilling lives. We want to know how to be satisfied.

God changes us if we let him. Ever since the world began, ordinary people have attained satisfaction—often in the worst circumstances known to man—by discovering God's purpose for their lives and living as they were meant to live.

The Four Stones changed my life. They will change yours too.

You have my guarantee.

The Parable of the Four Stones

PART 1
Life in Copyville

"Don't be late for dinner!" said Mrs. Livingstone. "I'm making your favorite tonight."

That could only mean one thing: spaghetti and meatballs. It had been Sam's favorite once, long ago. He pretended to like it as much as he always did. He didn't want to hurt his mother's feelings. Sam's parents wanted the best for him. They loved Sam and Sam loved them. But Sam's mind was made up. He knew what he had to do.

Mr. Livingstone was sure of the path he had taken in life. It would be the best path for Sam too. But Sam wasn't sure of that at all.

There were times when Sam walked into the house and caught a glimpse of his parents before they realized he was there. What he saw in their faces at moments like these was a kind of empty gaze, as if they were looking for something that wasn't there. It scared him. He wasn't sure why, but these moments made him feel uncomfortable for a long time. Not just for a few minutes, but for hours and days.

The Parable of the Four Stones

At other times Sam's parents seemed to be walking in their sleep, as if they weren't "all there." That was the best way Sam had found to express it, although he never talked about it to anyone. He tried to convince himself it was nothing to worry about. But there were times, thought Sam, when his parents seemed only half awake.

Sam had to be careful not to startle his parents at times like these. Mr. and Mrs. Livingstone didn't like surprises. They liked the kind of surprises that everyone likes: presents to open on Christmas morning and special friends who bring us something good to eat, like a chocolate cake or a banana pudding. But like all their friends, the Livingstones didn't like the kind of surprises that really surprise us.

People in Copyville liked predictable surprises, the kind that fit into the "not-so-surprising-after-all" category. But as everyone knows, there are two categories of surprises in life. Sam's parents didn't care for the second category: the sort of "surprises" that are impossible to predict.

The day the mill shut down is a perfect example of this kind of surprise. When the company built a new mill further upstream, Mr. Livingstone considered himself lucky to get a job there, even though it meant he would have to walk the extra distance to and from work each day.

Every morning Sam's father walked along the path that connected Copyville to Milltown, surrounded by other men who were fortunate enough to get jobs in the new mill. It wasn't so bad, Sam's father told himself. After all, he was one of the lucky ones. Not everyone in Copyville could say that.

Aside from the day the mill shut down, life in Copyville was comfortably predictable. That was its main attraction: A nice enough home in a nice enough corner of town with a nice enough income to feel far removed from the kind of surprises we would rather not think about. The Livingstones had these three things. Who could ask for more?

The Parable of the Four Stones

Sam Livingstone was just a child the day the mill shut down. It was the hardest year in the history of the Livingstone family. Some families left Copyville for good that year.

One of the families that left, the Anglers, were good friends of the Livingstones. John Angler was a fisherman. When the mill shut down the fish market was doomed. Most people had to get by on what they grew in their gardens. Some had livestock. No one could afford to buy fish anymore.

John came back to Copyville once, ten years after he left. The Anglers had a new life on the other side of the stream. John told everyone about the path he discovered.

"The path on the other side of the stream leads to a better life," John said.

"When are you going back?" Mr. Livingstone asked.

"I'm leaving tomorrow," said John. "You and your family are welcome to come with me."

Mr. Livingstone wasn't sure. "What will we do there? Where will we live? How will I make a living?"

John smiled. He had known Bill Livingstone since they were children. He knew it would take more than words to erase Bill's doubts.

"When we left we didn't have all the answers either," John said. "But we knew there was a better way. We had heard about it from others, but we had never seen it with our own eyes. Now I know. I've been there and back again. The path is real. If you go with me, you'll see it too."

"I can't answer all your questions right now or tell you what's going to happen tomorrow. But I can tell you this: Now that I've seen the other side of the stream, nothing on earth could keep me in Copyville."

Nothing on earth could convince Mr. Livingstone to leave Copyville. The next morning John Angler crossed the stream alone.

As he listened to John's stories, Sam tried to imagine what his life would be like on the other side of the stream.

"We're going with John in the morning, aren't we?" said Sam. "I can hardly wait!"

"Son, we need to have a talk," Mr. Livingstone said. That was all Sam needed to know. Whenever his father wanted to have a "talk" with him, it always meant the same thing: Sam would have no choice in the matter.

"Your mother and I have worked hard to have a place of our own," said Mr. Livingstone. "This house and land are all we have. It's too late for us to start over somewhere else."

"But Dad!" pleaded Sam.

"My mind is made up, Sam. It's the best thing for all of us. You'll feel better about it in the morning."

But Sam didn't feel better. He couldn't remember when he had felt so bad.

The next morning Sam went with John as far as the stream. The stream wasn't deep. Most adults were tall enough to wade across. But the undercurrent was treacherous; only fools went near the stream. Strong men had been sucked under by the current. Children in Copyville grew up listening to stories about men and women who tried to wade across and were never heard from again.

Standing on the bank, John pointed to four large stones that formed a kind of bridge. Each stone jutted out above the surface of the water. "This is the only way to cross the stream," he said.

Sam knew the place well. He was only a child the day two of his schoolmates dared him to skip across the stones.

"I'm not afraid," said Sam.

The stones were close enough together. It looked easy. A man could step from one stone to the next without having to leap. There was plenty of room for a man's foot to rest on the top of each stone. The four stones sparkled like diamonds as water splashed against them and threw spray high into the air.

"I'm not afraid," Sam said again. He stepped onto the first stone with his right foot. With his back foot planted on the bank of the stream, he didn't realize how slippery the stone was. He lifted his left leg and pushed off the first stone with his right foot.

Swoosh! Sam's right foot slipped on the smooth, wet surface. Spinning out of control, he fell—*Thud!*—hitting his head on the second stone. If his schoolmates hadn't grabbed his legs and pulled him out in the nick of time, Sam Livingstone would have gone down in history as the stream's youngest, and most foolish, victim.

"How did this happen?" Mrs. Livingstone asked, examining Sam's head. His parents had warned him, as all the townspeople warned their children, not to play near the stream.

"Sam, you could have been killed today," said Mrs. Livingstone, more startled than angry. "Promise me you won't go near the stream again. You can play on the path as much as you want. But promise me you won't go near the stream again."

Sam promised. But in his heart he knew he would cross the stream one day. Sam learned a lot that day. He had tried to skip across the stones without knowing how slippery they were. It would be different the next time.

The next time he would be prepared.

PART 2

Sam Finds a Friend

Sam Livingstone and John Angler stood on the bank of the stream.

"I wish I was going with you," said Sam.

John looked into Sam's eyes. "I wish everyone in Copyville was going with me," he said. "Everyone wants a better life. But most people don't know where to find it. When they run into an obstacle, like this stream, they change their direction and follow a different path."

"They tell themselves they have no choice. They follow a path they were never meant to be on. Before long, they stop thinking about the other path."

"I wish I was going with you," Sam said again.

"Your time will come," said John. "When it does, you'll need to remember everything I tell you today. Are you ready to learn how to be a Stream Crosser?"

"As ready as I'll ever be," answered Sam.

"To get to the other side you must know the stones," John said. "The stream is fast and the stones are slippery. Each stone is there for a reason. If you don't master the stones, the stream will defeat you. Stream Crosser Lesson Number

One: You're not ready to step onto the first stone until your vision is clear."

"There was nothing wrong with my eyesight the day I fell into the stream," said Sam. "My vision is perfectly clear."

John laughed. "Not as clear as you think, or you wouldn't have slipped on the first stone," he said. "The kind of vision I'm talking about has nothing to do with eyesight."

"What other kind is there?" said Sam.

"The kind that gives meaning to your life," explained John. "Your vision tells you where to go and why to go there."

"I knew where I wanted to go the day I fell into the stream," said Sam. "I wanted to go to the other side!"

"I would have guessed that much!" John said. "Wanting to get there isn't enough. You need a purpose that's big enough to carry you across. *Why* do you want to get there? Are you thinking only of yourself, or will your vision benefit other people? You must answer these questions before you step onto the first stone."

Sam was beginning to understand. "Wanting to impress my friends was a selfish reason," he said. "That's why I slipped on the first stone."

"That's right, Sam," said John. "You need a purpose that's bigger than yourself. If your purpose isn't something that benefits other people, it needs to be bigger."

Sam looked at the other bank. "I won't slip on the first stone the next time," he said. "Now tell me about the second stone."

"That should be easy for you, Sam Livingstone!" said John. "After all, it's written all over you."

"What's written all over me?" said Sam.

John put his hands on Sam's shoulders. "The second stone is your plan, Sam. It's not enough to know *what* you want to do. You have to know *how* you're going to do it. You

The Parable of the Four Stones

need a plan—specific, attainable, measurable steps that help you reach your destination."

"I don't get it," said Sam. "What's written all over me?"

John squeezed Sam's shoulders. "You can overcome any obstacle, starting with this stream, by taking specific, attainable, measurable steps."

Sam frowned. "I still don't get it," he said.

John spelled Sam's name, pronouncing each letter slowly and clearly. "S-A-M," said John, "specific—attainable—measurable steps."

Sam's eyes lit up. "Now I get it," he said. "I'll remember that!"

"Hey, Livingstone!" someone shouted. "Don't get too close to the edge! Dick and Steve aren't here to pull you out today." The jokes didn't bother Sam. But he was sorry John had to hear them.

Everyone in Copyville knew the story about Sam falling into the stream. The two boys that pulled him out were talented storytellers. It was their version of the near-fatal accident that found a place in local legend.

In their story, "crazy Sam Livingstone" started the whole thing by boasting he could jump across the stream. The boys cooked up their version of the story to "save our skin," as they put it.

"If my parents find out what really happened," said one of the boys, "I'm as good as dead."

"Yeah," added the second boy, "me too."

The boys got their story straight before they left the stream that day. This is the version their parents heard when the boys got home:

> Sam: *"Chickens! You guys might be afraid to cross the stream, but I'm not!"*

27

The Parable of the Four Stones

First Boy: *"Don't do it, Sam! You know how dangerous it is."*
Sam: *"I'm not afraid."*
Second Boy: *"Don't do it, Sam!"*
Sam: *"I'm not afraid."*

The boys told the rest of the story the way it really happened. After talking it over for what seemed like an eternity, they swore on the "graves of our great grandparents" never to "squeal on each other" even if "the whole town" believed Sam Livingstone's story.

They decided to leave Sam's "famous last words" intact. That was the "smart thing to do." If worse came to worse and everything blew up in their faces, the boys' thinking went, "sticking to the facts" was the best way to cover their tracks.

The boys saw the risk they were taking, but they figured there was safety in numbers: "Our word against his," as the first boy summed it up. "Two against one," added the other. This gave them the confidence they needed to return home that day.

The townspeople bought their story—lock, stock, and barrel. Sam's schoolmates were treated like heroes for pulling him out of the stream. Sam never told the real story to anyone, not even to his parents. The other boys could say what they wanted. Sam didn't care.

He wasn't ashamed of himself, even though everyone in town had decided by now that he was a "potential troublemaker." On the contrary, whenever Sam saw the other two boys he felt sure of himself—surer than he had ever been in his whole life. People talked about Sam behind his back. But *he* knew the truth.

Sam made a stupid mistake that almost cost him his life. The boys really did save Sam's life. But Sam wondered who had lost the most that day. He lost the respect of people who never questioned the falsified version. He couldn't deny that. But how much did his two friends lose? They knew the truth too.

Whenever Sam was around them, they seemed to be standing on pins and needles, as if they were waiting for something bad to happen. *How much have they lost?* Sam wondered.

A few weeks later, he had his answer. He wasn't even thinking about it when it came to him. *I might have lost the respect of some people,* Sam said to himself without knowing where the revelation came from, *but they lost their self-respect. Whatever I lost, I still have my self-respect.*

Standing on the bank of the stream that morning, another revelation was taking shape in Sam's mind. It shook his whole being: *I almost drowned that day, but they're still drowning. They need help now as much as I needed help that day.*

"Who needs help?" said John. "What are you talking about?"

Embarrassed by his absent-mindedness, Sam apologized. "It's nothing, John. I was just thinking out loud."

"A penny for your thoughts…"

"Really, it's nothing."

"Everything means something," said John. "When a thought comes from out of nowhere, God might be speaking to you. That's one of the ways he does it. Sam, do you believe in God?"

"I'm not sure. I mean—I don't know—I think I do."

"Whether you believe in him or not, he believes in you. He wants your attention. I'm not sure what it is, but I know he's speaking to you."

"If God was speaking to me, what would he say?"

"Most of the time he doesn't 'say' anything," John explained. "He speaks to us through the language of leanings, yearnings and even our imagination. He creates within

The Parable of the Four Stones

us the desire to discover our purpose in life. At different times in our life, Sam, he gives us visions—a clear understanding of what we're here for."

"You mean God can tell me what my purpose in life is? How could he do that?"

"Let me put it this way, Sam. If you have a vision for your life that isn't from God, you'll never be satisfied with anything life gives you. God created you for a purpose. You won't be happy until you discover what you're here for."

"What *am* I here for?" asked Sam, not so much because he expected John to have the answer, but because he was surprised to realize he had never really thought about it before.

"You're the only person who can know that, Sam. But I can tell you this: God created all of us for a reason. Think of it this way: One of the reasons you're here is to discover what you're here for."

"That's a riddle if there ever was one. Doesn't God have better things to do than think up riddles for people to solve?"

John grinned. "That's an interesting way to put it," he said. "For most people it is a riddle. Most people never figure it out as long as they live."

Sam wasn't sure if he had been standing next to John for minutes or hours. "Now I'm really confused," he confessed. "Why does God make it so hard? Why doesn't he come right out and tell us?"

"He does, Sam. Every time we read the Bible, he reminds us. The Bible is God's way of telling us what we're here for. It's the answer to every riddle."

"It might be the answer for you," said Sam, "but I still don't get it. I haven't read the Bible much, but I'm pretty sure it doesn't say whether I'm supposed to spend the rest of my life in Copyville or not."

The Parable of the Four Stones

"The Bible says more about that than you think, Sam Livingstone. It tells us not to copy the beliefs and behavior of the people around us. You probably never thought about it before, but why do you think they named this place Copyville?"

Sam hadn't thought about it before. Like everything else, it was just a name.

John had given Sam a lot of food for thought. Sam needed a few minutes to digest the meal.

"The Bible says that if we trust God, he'll help us discover our purpose in life," John explained. "God promises to guide us, but he won't force us. He only guides us if we let him. That's where visions come in. A vision is God's way of leading you."

"I think God just gave me a vision," said Sam. "Can I tell you about it before you leave?"

"I was hoping you would."

"Remember the time I fell in the stream?"

John smiled. "Sure," he said. "Who doesn't?"

"Well, you know the two boys who saved me? They really did save me, but it wasn't like they said it was. They dared me to cross the stream. I did it on a dare."

"I know it was a stupid thing to do, and it was my own fault, but I never would have done it if they hadn't dared me to. They were scared their parents would find out. I guess that's why they made up that lie about me."

"Go on," said John. "Tell me about your vision."

"Well, I was drowning that day—the day I fell in the stream. The boys that saved me are still drowning. They need help now, as much as I needed help that day. That was the vision I had, if you want to call it that."

"We're all drowning," replied John. "We're drowning when we're not on God's path. You see, there are only two paths you can take in life: God's path or your own path. Most people choose to follow their own path."

"God lets you decide which path to take. He won't stop you if you want to take your own path. But he won't forget you as long as you live. He'll always be waiting for you to change your path. He's waiting to show you the way now, Sam."

Sam closed his eyes. "Show me the way," he said. "Jesus, show me the way."

Sam opened his eyes. He looked all around. *This is what the world must look like to a newborn child,* he thought. He took a deep breath. "God doesn't want me to stay in Copyville, does he?"

"God doesn't want anyone to stay in Copyville," said John. "He's waiting for us to get on his path. See that path on the other side of the stream?"

"Of course I see it," answered Sam. "It's always been there. I never paid much attention to it."

John moved closer to Sam. They were standing shoulder to shoulder. John put his left arm around Sam. He straightened his right arm and pointed directly to the path.

"That's the answer to the riddle. That's what you're here for. It's what we're all here for; we're here to get on that path. What you see on the other side of the stream, Sam, is God's path for your life."

Sam looked down at the stream. "Then why did he put that here? If God wants us to get on his path, why did he make it so hard?"

"I don't have all the answers," John said. "But I know this: God always makes a way. When you want to follow his path with all your heart, he makes a way. That's why the stones are here."

Sam looked behind him for a moment. Then he looked at John again. "My parents are drowning too, aren't they?"

John nodded. "Yes, Sam," he said. "Everyone in Copyville is drowning. Everyone except you, that is—you just got saved."

The Parable of the Four Stones

"I know what I'm here for," said Sam. "I have to tell everyone. I have to tell them about the two paths. Then I have to... Wait a minute!"

"What is it, Sam?"

Sam looked down at the stream again. "I just remembered something. I'm still stuck on this side. I can't show other people how to get on God's path if I'm not on it."

"That's why the third stone is there, Sam. Lots of people reach the second stone. But that's as far as they get. As soon as they step onto the second stone, they try to jump all the way across. Nobody can do that. Nobody can make it without stepping onto the third stone."

Sam looked at the stone. "I know what the third stone is," he said. "I fell that day because I lost my balance. People always fall when they lose their balance. It doesn't matter how far you get. If you're out of balance, you won't make it to the other side."

"Bravo!" said John. "I couldn't have said it better. You can't get to the other side if any part of you is out of balance."

Sam studied the stones. He let his eyes move slowly from one stone to the next: vision, planning, balance. He had never really taken the time to look at them before.

"What's the last stone?" asked Sam.

John focused on the fourth stone. "From over here, it seems so close to the other side. How could anyone fail after getting that far? But the fourth stone is as far as some people get."

"I can't imagine a worse position to be in," said John. "A lot of people get stuck with one foot on the second stone and the other foot on the third stone. They can't stay that way forever. They lose their footing sooner or later. The stream will defeat you if you don't take the last step."

The Parable of the Four Stones

Sam didn't need to ask again. "So the last stone is action," he said. "Vision, planning, and balance can take you close enough to the other side that you can almost touch it. But you still have to take the last step."

"Well done, Sam!" John gave him a hearty pat on the back. "You're starting to turn into the leader God destined you to be."

"Leader?" said Sam. "I thought you said we're supposed to let God lead us."

John looked around for a way to make it clear. Sam had already solved more riddles in one day than some people solve in a lifetime. But he was too new to this business to know that some questions contain their own answers.

"Come over here," said John. "I want to show you something." John stopped at the foot of a birch tree. He had loved playing by the stream when he was a child. Caterpillars could be seen wiggling up tree trunks at this time of year. If John Angler had learned anything growing up in Copyville, it was that God's fingerprints are in these trees.

He soon found what he was looking for. "Do you see that?" he said. "It's hanging from a twig on the first branch."

Sam stared at the branch. "What do you mean? It's just a branch."

"Things are more than what they appear to be," said John, pointing to a trail of ants marching up the trunk.

"An ordinary birch tree, one you've walked by every day in your life, can reveal a piece of God's plan," John said. "You've walked by this tree thousands of times, but you've never really seen it."

Sam looked as hard as he could. Then he saw it. He had never seen a real cocoon before. He wasn't sure what it was at first. Then he realized he had always seen butterflies along the stream at this time of year. He hadn't thought about it for

The Parable of the Four Stones

a long time, but this was one of the places where he used to see lots of them.

"I see it now," said Sam. "It's a cocoon."

"And what's a cocoon?"

"Everybody knows what a cocoon is. It's where a caterpillar turns into a butterfly."

It was time for John to leave. He would need to choose his words well. Such a miracle of God's design and so little time to explain it!

"Everyone in Copyville is in the caterpillar stage," said John. He paused to let a picture form in Sam's mind. "They wiggle back and forth on the same path, but never go anywhere. Each day is like the day before. Their noses are too close to the ground to notice life on a different level."

"Until today, Sam, you were in the caterpillar stage. Now you're in a cocoon. You're turning into a new person. When you break out of your cocoon, you won't wiggle on the ground anymore. You'll soar on wings."

Sam looked at the cocoon again. "I'm not sure I understand. How could I be in a cocoon?"

"The cocoon is your own mind," explained John. "It's everything you believe. Think of it this way. A caterpillar's physical appearance changes inside a cocoon. The caterpillar doesn't engineer the change, but it has a part to play in God's plan. It finds a twig and builds a cage around itself. When the time comes, it struggles for hours to break out of its cage."

"God turns us into new persons by changing the way we think. Like the caterpillar, we don't engineer the change, but we have a part to play in the process. Our part is to leave our old thoughts behind. When we read the Bible, we start to think in a different way. In the end, things that mattered in the past aren't important to us anymore, and some things that used to seem silly are the most important things in life."

"Today is not the time to talk of endings. But the end of this story is a happy one. The Bible says we will be given

The Parable of the Four Stones

new bodies in heaven. But that's only half the story: God wants to give us new minds here on earth. Butterflies are God's way of saying, 'This is just a small preview of what I'm turning you into.' Can you see that, Sam? He's turning you into something beautiful."

Sam was beginning to see. He knew he wasn't created to live in Copyville. He was meant to soar, and soaring was only possible on the other side of the stream.

"Take me with you," said Sam.

"You're almost ready," John answered. "You've been a good learner today, but there's one more thing you need to learn. You won't be ready to leave Copyville until you learn how to lead yourself."

"Is that another riddle?" asked Sam. "It doesn't make sense."

"It will all make sense sooner than you think," said John. "For now, just remember this: You're leading yourself when you act your way into a feeling instead of feeling your way into an action."

John stepped across the stones and onto the path.

PART 3

Sam Solves a Riddle

John Angler's words stayed in Sam's head the rest of the day. *It will all make sense...*

"What will make sense?" asked Mrs. Livingstone. Sam was talking to himself again, this time at the dinner table.

"It's nothing, Mom," said Sam. "I was just thinking out loud." Then he remembered what John said at the stream that day. *Everything means something.* If God was speaking to him at the dinner table, thought Sam, his parents were probably supposed to hear it too.

Sam knew what he wanted to say, but he wasn't sure how to say it. "Mom, Dad... do you ever wonder what you're here for?"

"What we're here for?" said Mrs. Livingstone. "What do you mean, Sam?"

"I mean, do you know what your purpose in life is?"

"Of course we do," said Mr. Livingstone. "Is this a school assignment, Sam? If it is, you'd better get your notebook out and write our answers down."

"It isn't for school, Dad," Sam explained. "I just wanted to know."

"Well, now you know," said Mr. Livingstone.

The Parable of the Four Stones

Mrs. Livingstone took her husband's hand in hers. "Bill, what is our purpose in life? We've never really talked about it."

"How can you say that, Sara? We've been married for over twenty years."

"But we've never talked about it."

There was a long silence after that. If God was speaking to Sam's parents now, he seemed to have their attention. Sam wasn't sure whether he had asked the right question, but the answer was loud and clear.

Mrs. Livingstone moved closer to her husband and stroked his arm. "Sam's right," she said. "We should talk about this. As a family, I mean. We all need to know why we're here."

"Am I the only person in this family who hasn't gone nuts?" said Mr. Livingstone. "I know why I'm here. I've always known and always will. I'm here to put food on the table for the three of us. I'm a responsible member of the community. I paid for this house and land and raised a son. Most days I have more 'purpose' in my life than I can handle."

Mrs. Livingstone looked straight into her husband's eyes. "Bill, do you ever wonder if there isn't more to life than the path from Copyville to Milltown? Do you remember the walks we used to take before we got married? We used to go down to the stream, near the place where Sam tried to go across. There's a path on the other side. You used to point it out to me."

"You said you knew someone who crossed the stream and followed that path. You said he came back once. He tried to convince your parents to leave Copyville with him, just like John Angler tried to convince us to leave. When your father died, you said the only path for you was to go to work in the mill."

"We've been on that path since the day we got married, Bill. It's not the only path. We've heard about the other

The Parable of the Four Stones

one—the one you used to show me on the other side of the stream. Different people have told us it's a better path. We never listened to them."

"It's not too late to change the path we're on," Sara Livingstone said. "Let's go for a walk—all three of us. Let's go down to the stream. I haven't seen the path on the other side for years."

"Not tonight, Sara," Mr. Livingstone said. "I don't feel like going anywhere tonight. I've been on my feet all day long."

"All right, Bill," Sara said. "You'll go with me, won't you, Sam?"

Sam and Mrs. Livingstone left the house arm in arm. Soon they were humming one of their favorite songs. They laughed all the way to the stream and back. Sam couldn't remember the last time he felt so close to his mother, or so far from his father.

He thought about it all night long. Maybe, just maybe, thought Sam, I said the right thing after all.

Not tonight, Sara... I don't feel like going anywhere tonight... act your way into a feeling instead of feeling your way into an action... it will all make sense...

The words went round and round in Sam's head. If this is what it feels like to be in a cocoon, thought Sam, he didn't want to be in it much longer.

John said something about 'breaking out.' Sam tried to remember. He wished he had written it down.

"That's the answer!" he said, half shouting the words. "I've got to write everything down: my vision, my plan, what I'm here for, the four stones... The four stones! I've got to write it all down. Then I'll be ready to cross the stream. It's what John meant when he said I had to learn to lead myself."

The Parable of the Four Stones

Everything made sense, just like John said it would. The stream wasn't a problem anymore. It never was the problem. Sam could see that now.

He sat down at his desk and began to write. He wrote until the words stopped coming. When he finished writing, satisfaction surrounded him. No more thoughts raced through his head. No speeches from the previous day's conversations echoed in his brain.

For the first time in a long time, Sam fell asleep as soon as he put his head on the pillow.

Every morning Bill Livingstone walked to work with the same group of men. Six days a week, Monday through Saturday, Bill met the other Pathwalkers at the spot where Conformity Street ends and the Copyville-Milltown path begins. From there the path followed the same course as the stream.

There had never been a reason to build a bridge across the stream. "Who would want to go there?" people said. So instead of building a bridge to nowhere, the citizens of Copyville voted to improve the path.

Shade trees were planted on both sides to make travel as comfortable as possible. Rest stations were built at strategic intervals. These were nothing more than a bench and a roof at first, but they were welcome improvements at the time.

The path's real attraction was the Frequent Pathwalker Plan. At first the path was free to use. As more and more people used the path, it was obvious improvements had to be made. The path needed to be widened to accommodate the increase in traffic. In one of the most fiercely contested referendums in Copyville history, the townspeople voted, by the narrowest of margins, to install toll booths at each end of the path.

The Copyville Path Commission (CPC) was formed to manage all aspects of the business. The Commission's

The Parable of the Four Stones

first official act was to establish the Frequent Pathwalker Plan. Pathwalkers who logged 1,000 round trips were given Silver Walker status. Those who logged 2,000 became Gold Walkers, and those who logged 3,000 were rewarded with Platinum Walker status, the most coveted prize of all.

Frequent Pathwalker Convenience Stores soon replaced the old rest stations. Travelers had the opportunity to redeem mileage for prizes. Traffic increased so fast, in fact, that Copyville's first power plant was built to satisfy CPC's need for electricity. "WE LIGHT UP YOUR PATH" was the slogan CPC became famous for.

This morning, like every morning, Bill Livingstone met the other Gold Walkers at the Copyville toll booth. Of course they wouldn't always be Gold Walkers: Some of the men needed less than 100 round trips to become Platinum Walkers.

"If the Copyville mill had shut down a few years earlier, I'd be a Platinum Walker by now," a man in Bill's group said every morning as he paid his toll.

"You'll get there," Bill Livingstone always said.

But this time Bill didn't say anything as the men paid their tolls. He couldn't stop thinking about his wife's questions. *Do you ever wonder if there isn't more to life? It's not too late to change the path we're on...*

A CPC advertisement on the side of the path announced, "WE PUT YOU ON THE RIGHT PATH." On most days Bill only needed to read the ads on his way to work to feel confident that everything in his life was in the right place.

He didn't feel confident about anything today. Sam's questions tugged at his heart. *Do you ever wonder what you're here for?* What had gotten into the boy? What had gotten into the boy's mother? The two of them dancing and singing all the way to the stream and back. Bill knew he would hear about that from half the population of Copyville.

The Parable of the Four Stones

"Hey, Bill," said one of the men. "The Easter Parade isn't for another three months." "The Singing Livingstones are my favorites to win the talent contest at the Copyville Fair this year," said another.

Bill looked at their faces. He wondered why he hadn't noticed before. The life had gone out of those faces. They laughed and told jokes, but the life had gone out of their faces. For the first time in his life, Bill Livingstone felt out of place on the path. He had never missed a day of work. He was a model employee. He would be a Platinum Walker in another year. But for the first time in his life, none of that mattered anymore.

"I'm here to put food on the table... I paid for this house and land and raised a son. Most days I have more purpose in my life than I can handle."

Bill Livingstone had done many good things in his life. No one could take that away from him. *Why do I feel like I've wasted my life? Why do I feel so unsatisfied?*

The thoughts took Bill by surprise. "Why do I feel so unsatisfied?" he whispered.

"Hey, Bill," said the man next to him. "You're talking to yourself. If you don't watch out, you'll be singing in the street with the rest of your family." The men laughed a long time after that.

As they passed the last Frequent Pathwalker store, Bill noticed the familiar ad: "DON'T LET LIFE PASS YOU BY: REDEEM YOUR FREQUENT PATHWALKER MILES HERE." He couldn't hide from the truth any longer: Life *was* passing him by.

He had done everything a man is supposed to do in Copyville. But in spite of his house and land and family and Gold Walker membership card, a part of him was empty. Whatever it was, it was a part of him the Frequent Pathwalker store couldn't fill.

Mrs. Livingstone pulled a weed out of the garden. "We'll have good tomatoes this year," she said. "Sam, I've been

The Parable of the Four Stones

trying to remember something John Angler said the night before he left."

"I know," said Sam. "I've been trying to remember everything he said."

"He said something about being empty—something about God."

"I know what he said, Mom. I wrote it down last night."

"What was it?"

"He said, 'God made us to be empty without him.' He said we'll never be satisfied until we discover God's path for our lives."

Sam and his mother were sitting at the table when Mr. Livingstone got home. They had been talking a lot about John Angler.

"You're late," Mrs. Livingstone said. "Is everything all right at the mill?"

"Yeah, Sara, the mill's fine."

"What's wrong, Bill? You look like you just lost your best friend," said Mrs. Livingstone.

"I was thinking about John Angler on the way home. Something made me stop at the stream. I just needed to be alone for a while."

"I know why you stopped at the stream," Mrs. Livingstone said.

"How could you? You didn't even know I was there."

"But I know why you stopped," she said. "The night before John left, he said something: 'God made us to be empty without him.' That's why you stopped at the stream—because you're empty and you don't know what to do about it."

Mrs. Livingstone waited for her husband to say something. After a moment, she said, "I'm empty too."

Cocoon season, Sam said to himself. Cocoons were springing up all over the Livingstone household.

The Parable of the Four Stones

The waste basket next to Sam's desk was stuffed with crumpled sheets of paper. Sam had ripped most of the pages out of his writing tablet. He wrote the final draft as clearly as he could. The version below is the last thing he wrote before falling asleep.

WHAT I'M HERE FOR
(My purpose in life)
By Sam Livingstone

THE WRONG PATH
People on the wrong path (everyone who's still in Copyville) go through life without a purpose. The Copyville-Milltown Path is MY WRONG PATH.

THE RIGHT PATH
People on the right path (the Anglers, other families that left Copyville when the mill shut down) make decisions based on God's plan for their life. The path on the other side of the stream is MY RIGHT PATH.

MY 4 STONES

Stone #1: THE VISION*
Tell people about the two paths. Show them the 4 stones and teach them how to cross the stream (like John taught me). A big part of this is helping people understand that Jesus makes your life more satisfying. You will accomplish more with Jesus in your life than without him!

*To accomplish my vision, I need to change the way I think (in other words, I have to break out of my cocoon, because as long as I'm in it, it's a case of the blind leading the blind). I need to get on (and stay on) my right path. To get on the right path I need to make RIGHT CHOICES.

Stone #2: THE PLAN
The key to every good plan (easy for me to remember!) is **SAM**: Specific, Attainable, Measurable steps.

SAM'S SAM:
(1) Get ready to cross the stream (I'm doing that now)
(2) Cross the stream
(3) Get on my right path
(4) Find John Angler (if I don't find John, I'll find somebody else, after all, anybody who's on the right path should be able to tell me what to do next)
(5) Find out what to do next
(6) Do it
(7) Figure out what to do after that

Stone #3: BALANCE
(This is the hard one) I'm not sure about this one yet. I think it has a lot to do with making the right choices in every area of my life: the right choice about my path in life, the right choices about how I treat other people, the right choice about the person I marry, the right choices about the people I associate with *, eat the right food, take care of my body, etc.

*stay away from liars, cheaters, complainers, criticizers, blamers, gossipers

How to know when I'm leading myself:
I'm leading myself when I see a vision for my life; when I write it down as clearly as I can; when I set timelines for everything I want to do; when I set goals and plan how I'm going to reach them; when I remember to use the 4 stones every time I run into an obstacle (and when I don't run into obstacles, because I need the 4 stones all the time).

THE KEY THING TO REMEMBER ABOUT BALANCE IS: Everything is connected. Even when you're sure something isn't connected to something else, it is.

Stone #4: ACTION

I'll never discover GOD'S BEST FOR MY LIFE until I have a new mind. Right now I'm in the cocoon stage (Thank God I'm not a total caterpillar anymore) but for that to happen (discover God's best for my life) I have to get on my right path (the Copyville-Milltown path is NOT MY RIGHT PATH—the CPC ad says it is, but it's a lie).

I can't sit around and wait for the change to happen first and then cross the stream. I have to cross the stream and get on my right path first, then God will have something to work with (my new mind) so he can change the way I think and then I'll be able to lead the blind because I won't be blind anymore. I have to go now because if I don't, I'll never break out of my cocoon and (John didn't explain this part) I might be stuck in it for the rest of my life (but I'm not sure about this part).

MY NEXT ACTION:
CROSS THE STREAM! ASAP!

P.S. I'm ready to go because I have my vision and plan written down, I understand balance and ready to take action. That means I'm learning how to lead myself. John said I would be ready to go when I learned how to lead myself.

PP.S. I'm as ready as I'll ever be.

PART 4

Sam Starts a New Life

Sam's plan went without a hitch. As soon as he left home, he went to see Dick Defiant and Steve Sullen, the boys who pulled him out of the stream. Sam's old schoolmates lived on the same street. It wouldn't be hard to find them.

Sam went to Steve's house first. He wasn't surprised when Dick opened the door. Dick and Steve were as close to being inseparable as any two people Sam had ever known. Dick and Steve kept Sam waiting for several minutes before joining him on the front porch.

"This won't take long," said Sam. "I only have a minute."

"Sixty seconds and counting," said Dick.

"Your minute's down to fifty-five seconds," said Steve. "Like you said, this won't take long."

"Fifty seconds and counting," said Dick, pointing at the second hand on his wristwatch.

Sam felt sorry for his old schoolmates. If caterpillars could speak, thought Sam, they would sound like Dick and Steve.

"I came here to thank you for saving my life," said Sam. "I should have done it a long time ago."

Sam looked straight into Dick's eyes. "Thank you for saving my life, Dick," he said. Dick was too shocked to know what to do.

Sam looked at Steve. "Thanks for pulling me out of the stream, Steve. You saved my life."

Sam let the boys regain their composure. He figured it would take a minute. He already knew what he was going to say next. "Dick... Steve... I need you to do something for me."

Sam handed Steve an envelope. "Could you give this to my parents? It's important."

"What's going on, Sam?" said Steve. "What's this all about?"

Sam handed Steve a second envelope. "This is for you and Dick. When you read it, you'll understand."

Sam walked down the porch steps. Then he turned and said, "You guys would look good in cocoons."

Sam smiled and hurried away.

A few minutes later, Sam was standing on the bank of the stream. He looked at the four stones. "Vision, plan, balance, action," he said. "I won't fall this time."

Sure of himself, Sam stepped across the first three stones with confidence. His movements were neither too fast nor too slow. Every part of him was in balance.

Up to this point, everything had gone exactly as Sam planned it. Then, for no obvious reason, he hesitated. *This is the worst position I could be in*, thought Sam. He stared at the stream. The water was moving faster.

The stream was rising: It would be over the top of the stones soon. Sam's legs ached. His calves felt as tight as a screw. *I'll never reach the bank if my legs cramp up. How did I get in this position?*

For a moment, Sam wasn't sure he was going to make it. Then something happened. Sam took a deep breath. As he

The Parable of the Four Stones

did, he caught himself wishing John Angler was there to grab his hand and pull him to the other side. Thinking of John was all Sam needed to remember what he already knew.

"I still have to take the last step," he said at last.

As soon as he spoke the words, Sam stopped thinking about his legs. He stopped thinking about the position he was in. He stopped thinking about the stream. He focused all his attention on the next movement he was going to make. He was ready to make a superhuman effort to throw himself onto the bank.

Sam lifted his left foot off the third stone. As he pushed off the last stone with his right foot, the momentum created by this simple movement carried him safely onto the bank.

"That wasn't hard," said Sam. Then, realizing what he had accomplished, he let it all gush out. "I made it! I made it! I made it!"

Sam lifted his arms as high as he could. He tilted his head back. He let his eyes feast on the sight for a moment. "Thank you, Jesus," he said. "I couldn't have made it without you."

He had one more thing to do. Kneeling next to the fresh footprints, he picked out a nice, sharp stone and carved a sign into the bank of the stream. Then he ran onto the path and disappeared around the first bend.

"What do you think?" said Dick.

"I'm not sure what to think right now," said Steve.

Dick scratched the top of his head. "What was that crack about cocoons supposed to mean?"

"Your guess is as good as mine," said Steve. "We'll have time to figure that out later." He held up the first envelope to remind Dick of their mission. "We have to take care of this first."

"Right," said Dick. "Let's go."

It didn't take Dick and Steve long to reach the stream. The first thing they saw was the sign: "V" for Victory. It was right where Sam said it would be.

Mrs. Livingstone opened the door. After the initial shock of seeing Dick Defiant and Steve Sullen standing on her property, she was finally able to say, "Well, boys... what can I do for you?"

"Sam told us to give you this," said Steve, handing her the envelope.

"Everything's O.K., Mrs. Livingstone," said Dick. "Sam's fine. When you read that, you'll understand."

"Don't worry, Mrs. Livingstone," said Steve.

"Everything's O.K.," Dick said again.

The boys crossed the street and sprinted out of sight.

It wouldn't take long to find John Angler. A man tending a flock of sheep on the side of the path told Sam everything he needed to know.

"Hello, Sam," said the man.

Sam was getting used to surprises. He was pleased to discover how much he liked being surprised. "How do you know my name?" he asked.

"People on this path know more than you think, Sam Livingstone," said the man.

Sam decided it would be fun to give the man a surprise of his own. "What else did John Angler tell you about me?"

"Nothing I couldn't have figured out myself," said the man.

"In that case, I'm sure you'll be happy to tell me where to find him," to which Sam added, "Mister...?" He let his voice trail off long enough for the man to get the point.

"Shepherd," said the man. "You can call me Shepherd."

"Does that mean you're Mister Shepherd, or are you just a shepherd?"

The Parable of the Four Stones

"People are more than what they appear to be, young man. Didn't John Angler teach you that?"

Sam didn't mind being talked to in riddles. Not anymore, that is. To tell the truth, he was tired of living in a place whose main attraction was its predictability.

"Yes, John taught me that," said Sam. "You must be Mister Shepherd, the shepherd, who's here to shepherd me."

Mister Shepherd, the shepherd, rewarded Sam with a friendly wink. "Now you're ready for the next stage of your journey."

According to Mister Shepherd's calculations, Sam would reach John's house by sundown. Sam winked at Mister Shepherd as he turned back to the path. He arrived at John's house just in time for dinner.

From Sam's point of view, dinner ended much too soon, for seated next to Sam was Angela Angler, who had turned into a beautiful young woman in the ten years since the Anglers left Copyville.

Sam kept the after-dinner conversation going as long as he could. He even offered to help with the dishes. (Angela, of course, was already in the kitchen putting on her apron when Sam so generously offered to help.)

John took Sam for a walk along the path. "If I know my daughter," he said, "you'll have plenty of opportunities to help with the dishes."

John and Sam looked at the mountains ahead. "The Mountains of Meaning," said John, pronouncing the words as if they were the answer to all of Sam's questions.

"Everyone in Copyville is searching for those mountains. More people would cross the stream if they knew how near those mountains are. It doesn't take long to reach them when you're on the right path."

John pointed to the tallest mountain. "The Peak of Satisfaction," he said.

"I see the one you mean," said Sam.

"This path leads straight to it," John said. "If people only knew..."

Sam looked at the mountains. Then he looked back down the path.

John knew what Sam was thinking. "God wants everyone to reach that peak," he said. "He made this path to guide us. You're going to run into obstacles. There are wider streams to cross than the one in Copyville. But they're not the real obstacle."

"The only obstacle that can defeat you is a different kind of stream—the stream that roars inside your own head, telling you to be afraid, telling you to doubt yourself, telling you there's no hope. When you hear that stream, look at those mountains and remember where your help comes from."

John let the message sink in. Then he said, "You'll stay with us tonight."

"I'll need to get an early start in the morning," said Sam. "If everything goes according to plan, four people will break out of their cocoons tomorrow."

Then he added, "I don't want to miss it!"

The next morning Sam thanked Mrs. Angler for her hospitality. John gave Sam a present. "You'll need this," he said.

Sam took the gift in his hands. "Dick and Steve weren't the only ones who saved me," he said. "You saved me too, John."

"Let's just say I played a part in the Engineer's plan," John replied.

Sam turned around one last time. The Angler home was too far away to see. He knew what John meant: We don't engineer the change, but we have a part to play in it. Sam understood what that meant.

The Parable of the Four Stones

But at the same time, it was a mystery. How can you understand something, he wondered, yet not understand? It was a question Sam would be sure to ask the next time he saw John Angler.

He sat down on a smooth stone beside the path and unwrapped the present. When he realized what it was, he said, "I needed this sooner than you thought, John Angler."

Sam opened the Book and took out his pen. It was an important question. He wanted to write it down in a place where he would be sure to find it. He turned the page, looking for a good place to write a note to himself.

When he found John's note, he smiled. John might have been the best fisherman in Copyville at one time, thought Sam, but he could use a few spelling lessons:

HOLY BIBLE
*To Sam, living stone
From John, fisher of men*

There was more. Was this another one of John's riddles? It might have been written in ancient code for all Sam could make of it. Sam was so new to the Book; he didn't know what it was at first. John's strange message, which turned out to be coded after all, was pointing to a passage in the New Testament:

$$==l\sim o\sim o\sim 1\sim Pe\sim 2\sim o\sim o\sim l==$$

Sam found the passage, but the first thing he read was the handwritten note at the bottom of the page:

*On This Rock, a living stone is born.
Remember who the Engineer is, and play your part well.*

The Parable of the Four Stones

Sam read John's note over and over. He wasn't sure what it meant. Sam closed the Book. An almost imperceptible breeze brushed against his arm. A host of butterflies appeared from out of nowhere. *There must be thousands of them,* thought Sam. Two or three fluttered right in front of Sam's nose before the whole host vanished as quickly as it had appeared.

With the Book under his arm, Sam stood up and started down the path as the last flying caterpillars disappeared into the forest. "Oh, no!" he exclaimed, coming to an abrupt halt. "I didn't find out what to do next."

Then he got it: John had already given him the answer. He was holding it in his hands.

CHAPTER 1

What We Ought to Be

*"Compared with what we ought to be,
we are only half awake."*
—*William James*

The Four Stones is a story of spiritual awakening. "Mr. Livingstone was sure of the path he had taken in life. It would be the best path for Sam too. But Sam wasn't sure of that at all."

As the story begins, Sam senses that something is wrong in the Livingstone household. At times his parents have an "empty gaze" in their eyes, "as if they were looking for something that wasn't there." Sam is beginning to realize that his parents aren't "all there." Mr. and Mrs. Livingstone are only half awake.

The Four Stones is the story of a young man's journey from half awake to fully awake. When we discover that we have the ability to set and accomplish goals, we begin to approach everything we do in life with a new sense of purpose. We become what we ought to be.

Sam's story shows how important it is to: (1) get a *vision* for our life; (2) design a *plan* to accomplish the vision; (3)

establish *balance* in all areas of our life and plan; and (4) take *action* to achieve our vision.

The lesson of *The Four Stones* is a simple one: True satisfaction is only possible when we get on, and stay on, God's path for our life. The path is open to everyone, but it requires us to make good choices. We must bring our thoughts into alignment with God's vision for our life and take the right steps to accomplish the vision.

I wrote this book to show, step by step, how easy it is to implement *The Four Stones* in your life. Many books have been written about the "purpose" process: Vision, Plan, and Action are all areas of achievement that have been taught in detail. A fourth dimension, Balance, has been left out of the picture. My book adds this new dimension to the process.

A major theme of *The Four Stones* is personal leadership: leading yourself to make good decisions and to take planned, balanced actions. You're leading yourself when you see a vision for your life; record that vision clearly in words; set timelines; make plans; and keep your life in balance.

Another theme of *The Four Stones* is the idea that there are only two paths in life. In Sam's story, they take the form of the Copyville-Milltown path and the path on the other side of the stream. People on the first path allow circumstances to dictate the direction they take in life; they live by default. People on the second path allow God to determine the direction they take; they live by design.

Living by default is the path of least resistance: People on this path go through life without a plan or purpose. Living by design is a path of choice: People on this path have discovered God's purpose for their lives.

The First Stone

Vision, Plan, Balance, and Action are God-given support mechanisms that help us overcome obstacles. In Sam

Livingstone's story, these mechanisms are represented by four stones in a stream. The stream represents the obstacle.

The first stone is *vision*. To overcome any obstacle we must first have a clear vision of what we expect on the other side. This is a personal choice—a choice we must make consciously for ourselves. Without a clear vision, we can't expect to find the path of God's best on the other side of the obstacle. Without a vision, we're likely to lose our footing and fall into the stream.

Obtaining a clear, personal vision for our life can be overwhelming if we aren't used to making choices for ourselves. A good starting place is to identify where we are in life. In *The Four Stones*, people run into a dead-end when they come to the stream. Looking to their right, they see a wide path. It's smooth and easy, but it takes them away from where they thought they were headed. This is the path of distraction: People on this path let others make decisions for them by default.

The same thing happens to us. We thought we were on a path for our life. Now we must make a choice: We allow life to change our path or we make a conscious decision to find a way past the obstacle.

As we stand on the bank of the stream, the water rushes by too fast for us to wade across. We aren't sure how deep the stream is. Taking a second look, we notice four small stones. The stones are wet from the overspray of the rushing water. We can cross the stream if we take deliberate steps to maintain our footing. Each stone is only large enough for one foot. To overcome the obstacle, we must make a choice about our future.

The safe choice is to follow the path of default. This path takes us away from where we thought we wanted to go in life. We had dreams once: We dreamed about going places, accomplishing goals, and having things. Now and then we meet people who do what they want. They've accomplished what we wanted to accomplish and have what we wanted to have. They're doing something different, but what is it? These people—the ones that seem to be doing something different—represent only 3% of the population. They're living life by design.

On the other side of the stream we see the path that takes us in the direction we had always dreamed of going. Standing at the stream's edge, we can reach the first stone if we're willing to try. People pass by as they go down the path of default. They encourage us to join them.

Though they wish us well, they feel threatened by our choice of a different path. They may even want us to fail, though they usually keep this a secret. If we can step out onto the first stone, our clear vision will define our choices and strengthen our resolve. On the other hand, we'll be alone—responsible for the choice we made. Is it worth the risk?

We step out onto the first stone. It's small and slippery. The fast-moving stream splashes onto the stone. Wet spray lands on our foot. With our right foot securely planted on the Stone of Vision, we balance ourselves in the middle of our obstacle.

Even though the spray is swirling all around us, our vision becomes clear. With one foot on the Stone of Vision, we learn an important lesson: The choice we made to pursue our vision is rewarding us with clarity.

With the fast-moving stream all around us, we have two choices. We can reach for the next stone or turn around and go back. If we go back there is safety in numbers. If we go forward we will have to make even more choices to accomplish our vision. In order to move forward, we must have a plan. Designing a plan to accomplish our vision requires additional choices. There is no one else to blame if we make the wrong choice.

Our vision is a clear picture of our desire—the thing we long to do the most. We begin to envision ourselves accomplishing a specific dream for our life. We understand more now than we did before we took the first step.

In the past, we were easily pushed onto a path of default because our vision was too general: Everything seemed right at the time. We allowed choices to be made for us because we didn't have a clear picture of where we wanted to go.

Standing on the Stone of Vision in the middle of our obstacle, we learn a second lesson: The only way to accomplish our vision is to have a clear mental image of what our life will be like when we achieve our dream. Our vision has moved from a general thought to a specific, attainable, and measurable goal. We hold a picture of the goal in our mind as we visualize the outcome we desire.

The Second Stone

The second stone is further out into our obstacle. This is the Stone of Plan; it's there to give structure to our life. To move our vision forward we must develop a plan. The plan will guide us through our obstacle and propel us toward the path of God's best.

Now that our vision is clear, we can create a plan—our personal roadmap—to accomplish the specific, attainable, and measurable picture we have for our future. We need a well-planned roadmap to measure our progress: It tells us how far we've come and how far we still have to go to reach our vision.

Developing our plan requires us to make choices. It's not too late to return to the other path. Life seemed easier on the path of default, though it was full of dissatisfaction. Thanks to our clear, personal vision, life has taken on new meaning. We look forward to every day with renewed enthusiasm and hope. We don't want to turn back now. Let's go for it!

We take a huge second step and land on the Stone of Plan. As our left foot rests on the wet stone, we realize how close we are to falling into the stream. The third stone is to our left. We can reach it, but we'll be out of position for our next step. The fourth stone is too far to reach by leaping all the way from the second stone. We dare not switch feet on any of the four stones; the risk of slipping is too high.

After a quick evaluation, the only choice is to go back to the shore. The frustration of going back makes us question our purpose. How do we even know we had the right vision for our life? Maybe the others were right. Maybe I should have stayed on the path of default. Maybe others are making the right choices for me.

No. We're going back to regain the proper alignments. As leadership strategist Keith Craft says, "Alignment comes before assignment."

Going back doesn't change our vision. This delay allows us to clarify our vision. We're now in a position to make better choices based on recent experiences and to align our steps for greater progress. We step cautiously back to the Stone of Vision and jump onto dry land.

Making Choices

Back on the shore of default, we're greeted by the "I-told-you-so" well-wishers. Fear, Uncertainty, and Doubt, our old friends, encourage us to continue on the path of default. A simple turn, a few steps, and we'll be cured of our temporary insanity—our belief that we can live by design.

"If people were meant to live by design," we tell ourselves, "more of us would be doing it."

Once again, we face a choice. Following our vision requires us to step out into the obstacle, where we assume full responsibility for making the right choices. We can always fall back on the easy path of default and distraction. Taking a deep breath, we lead with the left foot this time and leap onto the first stone.

The Parable of the Four Stones

In spite of the wet, slippery surface and the fast-moving stream that sprays mist onto our foot, we once again gain a clear vision for our future. Few people get this far: We see a clear picture for our life and get excited about the new possibilities.

Once again, our clear vision prompts us to move onward to the second stone, the Stone of Plan. More choices await us: We must deal with being responsible for those choices. If we choose to go forward, we will have nobody else to blame for our mistakes.

Taking another deep breath and another big step, our right foot lands on the Stone of Plan. It is now time to make the plans which will move us closer to the path of God's best.

The idea of creating a roadmap for our life is overwhelming. We're getting tired of standing on this small wet stone in the middle of our obstacle. The rush of the obstacle against the stone makes us uncomfortable. Should we go back to the shore of default again? Have we made the wrong choice by trying to live our vision?

No. We only need to make a few small choices. First, we need to develop our plan well enough to land us on the path of God's best. We can evaluate and modify our plan as soon as we move beyond this obstacle.

We need our roadmap once again: specific, attainable, and measurable steps to keep us moving toward the other shore. Our confidence grows with every step we take.

The Third Stone

The third stone, Balance, is within reach of our left foot. We can reach it without pulling our other foot off the second stone. The fast-moving stream pounds against the third stone. As we stretch to reach the third stone, will we slip and fall? It doesn't look too risky, so we extend our left leg and place it on the third stone.

We are now secure with one foot on the Stone of Plan and the other on the Stone of Balance. Even though the obstacle rushes beneath us, we're safe for the moment. We check our choices and put the finishing touches on our plan.

Our feet are planted on the second and third stones. In a place of plan and balance, we can build up our confidence as the obstacle rushes beneath us. We take time to develop our plan and make sure our life is in balance. We evaluate our plan and visualize the next step. We establish priorities and draw up the specific, attainable, and measurable steps that are the backbone of every successful plan.

Why do we need specific, attainable, and measurable steps? Specific steps help us determine our risk: How much will it cost to take the next step? Can I afford to take it? Can I afford not to take it?

Our vision is written in a place where we can see it. In the words of Keith Craft, "We say what we hear so we can see what we say." Our roadmap reminds us to take small steps. Our confidence is growing; it's time to move. The obstacle is coming faster. We can't stay in the same place much longer.

The Fourth Stone

The fourth stone, Action, is a long stretch from the Stone of Balance. It isn't too late to go back to the shore of default. Fear, Uncertainty, and Doubt tell us it wouldn't be so bad to turn around.

With a clear vision for our future, we press on to the shore of our dreams. Our plan is a good plan; our roadmap gives us a specific, attainable, and measurable route to follow. All we need to do now is take the next step to reach the Stone of Action. This is no time to look back: We're close to the path of God's best. Here we go...

Our right foot lands squarely on the Stone of Action. As soon as our foot touches the stone, we feel motivated and energized. We have new hope for our future. One small step has given us a sense of accomplishment—something we haven't felt in a long time. We feel good because we acted our way into a feeling.

Why did we take that step? Was it for money, security, or acceptance? Was it for self-esteem? We took the step because of our sense of purpose.

We have a vision for our future that requires us to move forward in small steps. Our plan calls for small, specific steps that are attainable and measurable. Standing on the Stone of Action, we have made a step toward our vision. Our confidence is soaring. We're only one step away from the shore of God's best.

The obstacle is still raging around us, but it doesn't seem so big any more. Just one more step and it will be behind us. What about our friends on the other shore? Who will we blame for our choices if we fail now?

We're almost there. We can make it if we establish our priorities, accept responsibility for our decisions, and make a commitment to base our lives on the things that matter most to us.

Our foot touches the new shore of God's path for our life. We give thanks for the new sense of accomplishment; for the strength to overcome this obstacle; and for the wisdom to make the right choices.

We've learned to be responsible for our choices and to live by design. There will be other obstacles in our path, but we know we can overcome them by holding onto our vision and making the right choices.

The right choices are the ones that help us accomplish our vision. When we know where we want to go, we can design a plan and take appropriate actions to get there.

As we step onto the path of God's best, we realize our priorities were wrong in the past. We were focused on money first, then career and family. If we had any time left after taking care of the first three areas, we focused on our health. We allowed our career to take time away from our family.

Now that we're living life by design, it's time to redefine our priorities. Maintaining proper balance in our lives is essential to our health and well-being. Our new focus should be on our spiritual time, our attitude, and our body. When we make these areas our top priorities, we bring our lives into alignment with our God-given purpose. Our other priorities must be family, career, and financial goals—in that order.

We refine our vision for the future on the basis of our new priorities. We continually renew our vision as we become more enthusiastic about the possibilities that each day offers. We continually review and update our plans to keep moving closer to the goals we envision. Taking small action steps keeps us motivated. As we begin to fulfill our purpose, life is more satisfying.

Vision, plan, and actions change over time. Renewing our vision keeps us on the path of God's best by keeping our goals in alignment with God's purpose for our lives.

Even on the path of God's best, there will be obstacles to overcome. We can avoid many obstacles by making better choices. But even though you make the best choices, you may still run into obstacles. The key to overcoming them is to stay on God's path, maintain your vision, update your plan, and take appropriate actions.

The 'Code' in the Stones

In Part 4 of *The Four Stones*, John teaches Sam one last lesson:

> There are wider streams to cross than the one in Copyville. But they're not the real obstacle. The only obstacle that can defeat you is a different kind

The Parable of the Four Stones

of stream—the stream that roars inside your own head, telling you to be afraid, telling you to doubt yourself, telling you there's no hope. When you hear that stream, look at those mountains and remember where your help comes from.

There will be seasons in life when Fear, Uncertainty, and Doubt visit us. At these times we must remind ourselves that we made a choice to follow a different path—a path of God's best.

We see now that these old acquaintances are our worst enemies. They're no longer welcome in our lives. Like Sam, we have learned the most valuable lesson of all: We have the power to choose who we listen to.

The Four Stones are real in my life. As a writer, speaker, and consultant, my goal is to: (1) Educate, (2) Empower, and (3) Mentor people to succeed. I call it "E^2M." My personal vision is to show people how to live rewarding and satisfying lives.

In *The Four Stones*, Sam discovers his purpose in life and follows the path of God's best. He begins the journey back to Copyville fully awake to the possibilities that life offers. Now that Sam's eyes are open, he wants to help other people open theirs. The first thing he opens is the present John Angler gave him.

He smiles as he reads the dedication: He thinks John is a bad speller. John's "coded" message leads Sam to a passage in the New Testament:

> You are coming to Christ, who is the living cornerstone of God's temple. He was rejected by people, but he was chosen by God for great honor. And you are living stones that God is building into his spiritual temple (1 Peter 2:4-5).

The Bible reveals Sam's true identity: He came into the world as Sam Livingstone, but he was meant to be a living stone.

And so were we.

The Two Paths: A Case Study

"The lab is a place for the young, and returning there you feel young again: with the same longing for adventure, discovery, and the unexpected that you have at seventeen."
—Primo Levi

Chemistry is an unadventurous subject for most students. Maybe I should say "boring." Few young people have as much passion for studying chemistry as they have for text messaging their friends.

Not many adventure stories have been written about chemists. Can you think of any off the top of your head? If you can't, don't feel bad. The mere mention of the word "chemistry" makes most people think of a laboratory technician in a white coat peering into a microscope. How adventurous can that be?

I was 19 when I went to work in an Exxon refinery laboratory in Baytown, Texas. As a shift worker at the refinery, I had the opportunity to study chemistry. Actually, the classes were required and I attended one class per week before or after my shift. My classes were taught by staff from the University of Houston. I was told that I would receive a Bachelor of Science degree when I completed the course work. I worked hard at achieving the required scores and completing the course work.

A few months before graduation I received disappointing news. Instead of a degree in chemistry, I would be given a Certificate of Completion as a Laboratory Technician. Although I completed the equivalent of a Bachelor's degree,

I wasn't rewarded for my effort. That is the closest I came to a degree.

Even that could not dampen my enthusiasm for the job; I was longing for adventure, discovery, and the unexpected. I loved my job, I was challenged and was rewarded for my successes.

A Mysterious Death

Did you think of an adventure story written about a chemist? If you haven't thought of one yet, you probably didn't see *The Rock*. In this 1996 box-office hit, Nicolas Cage plays the role of an FBI biochemist whose mission is to stop a deranged Marine commander (Ed Harris) from launching a chemical attack against the city of San Francisco.

The Rock is just a movie, of course. How exciting is the day-to-day life of real chemists when they aren't saving the world from terrorists? More exciting than you think: Chemistry can be the greatest adventure of all for those who love to unlock the secrets of the universe.

Primo Levi was such a person. He graduated from Italy's Turin University in 1941 with a degree in chemistry, but his diploma gave him little reason for hope. It was awarded to "Primo Levi, of the Jewish race." When Hitler's army occupied Italy in September, 1943, the 24-year-old Italian Jew went into hiding with a group of friends. A Gestapo spy infiltrated the group. Levi was captured 12 days before Christmas.

He was sent to the Auschwitz death camp in Poland, where he worked in a Nazi chemical plant. He had to learn how to steal to survive. The skills needed for survival in Auschwitz didn't come easily to Levi. Like all Jewish children, he had been taught the Ten Commandments.

Thou shalt not steal.

Even though he was starving, months passed before he got over the feeling that it was wrong to steal. Out of hunger and desperation, he ate sanitary cotton which he fried on an electric hot plate in the chemical lab where he worked.

Unlike millions of European Jews who died in Nazi death camps during World War II, Levi was a scientist. His captors kept him alive. In 1945, nearly dead of starvation, Levi was liberated by Russian troops.

"Perhaps it is true," he wrote many years later, "that there exists a God who protects children, fools, and drunks?" (Primo Levi, *The Periodic Table,* translated by Raymond Rosenthal: Schocken Books, 1984)

Levi never found the answer to his question. After the war, he had a successful career as a chemist in his native Italy. Through his books he became an international celebrity. His life seemed to be a testimony of the power of the human spirit to overcome evil. It ended mysteriously on April 11, 1987, when Levi fell from the inside landing of his third-floor apartment in Turin.

The coroner ruled it a suicide. Levi didn't leave a suicide note; his death might have been accidental. We will never know for sure. When fellow Holocaust survivor and Nobel Peace Prize winner Elie Wiesel heard the news of Levi's death, he offered a simple eulogy: "Primo Levi died at Auschwitz."

When Life Loses Meaning

We all have a path in life. From the moment of our birth until our last breath, we are on a path. For most of us, the path takes what seems to be a natural course. At an early age we show signs of success in some endeavor and we are immediately cast into a role. This role takes many shapes, has many expressions, and seems good to us and good for us.

Our role may change several times throughout our life. As we move into adulthood, our path takes new turns and twists. New experiences and opportunities shape our world. People around us speak expressions which feel good to our ears and seem appropriate to the path we are following.

The path is working out for us in a natural, expected way. Sure, we have obstacles in our path just like everyone else. The obstacles serve to redirect us along our path. Our friends encourage us and we have many things in common.

Every once in a while we meet people who are different. They seem to have more than other people—a level of satisfaction in their lives that the rest of us haven't attained. Their families are happier. They have a balance about them which we envy yet don't take the time to understand.

They're just special: They probably have rich parents and come from a background of money. If we just had more money we would be happier and more satisfied too!

It is estimated that 97% of us live life without a plan. This is the path of default, the most traveled road in the world. People who live life by default walk out their assigned life's path as long as nothing is in their way. When they run into an obstacle, they turn off their assigned path and follow a path of distraction. This sets off a continual cycle of frustration. Fear, Uncertainty, and Doubt—our constant companions on this path—tell us it's useless to hope for more.

Consciously or unconsciously, most people in the world choose to follow a path of default. Maybe they're distracted by something that looks good to them at their moment of choice. At other times they're pushed down the path of default because they allow others to make choices for them.

Either way, 97 of every 100 inhabitants of the planet follow a path that takes them farther and farther away from the life they wish they were living—the life they would live if they knew they could choose their own direction.

Primo Levi followed a path that led to a level of success beyond the wildest dreams of the man whose only goal had once been to steal enough food to survive. Yet in spite of his success and fame, he never found true satisfaction. He struggled with depression long before his life literally crashed to the ground in 1987.

Whether Levi's death was a suicide or an accident, his books make one thing clear: His life was a constant battle against depression and despair. Elie Wiesel was right: In a very real sense, Primo Levi never left Auschwitz.

When Life Is Worth Living

We encounter obstacles for many reasons. Most obstacles are the result of choices we have made in life. For every obstacle we encounter there is a new opportunity to make a choice. Either we choose to follow the path of default and distraction or we find a way to overcome the obstacle.

On the other side of an obstacle is a path of God's best for our life. This is the road less traveled. It's a path of vision, planning, balance, and action. Primo Levi had a clear vision for his life, first as a chemist and then as a writer. He planned his life, before and after Auschwitz, and acted on his plan. He achieved success in two different careers.

The path that Levi chose makes sense to most people. What could be more satisfying than pursuing two different careers—two jobs you love with all your heart, mind, and soul—and being successful at both? To most people that sounds like the good life. How could you fail to find happiness and satisfaction by following such a path?

We will never know whether the writer, chemist, and Holocaust survivor lost his balance and fell by accident or jumped to his death because his life had lost meaning. Whether or not Levi lost his balance at the top of the stairwell that day, he had been out of balance for a long time.

This is the lesson that Mr. and Mrs. Livingstone learn in *The Four Stones*: We live life out of balance until we understand that God made us for a purpose. Primo Levi made many discoveries during his life, but he never discovered the one thing that could have repaired his damaged spirit: a relationship with Jesus Christ.

When something is out of balance it can't function properly. Without balance, tires don't roll the way they should. Unbalanced tires cause wheels to get out of alignment. The ride is rough; the tires wear unevenly. Just as balance is a key to safe driving, it's also a key to a healthy, wealthy life.

No matter how successful a person seems to be, a life without Christ is a life without balance. The Bible says we're spiritually dead unless we receive Christ as our Savior. Vision, planning, and action can lead to fame and fortune, as they did in Primo Levi's case. But without the balance that only comes when the Spirit of God lives in a human heart, true satisfaction remains beyond our grasp.

Jesus wasn't popular with the religious authorities of his day. His words were a double-edged sword that offended and enraged the kind of people who hear only what they want to hear. But the same words that enraged the Pharisees gave new life and renewed hope to everyone who received Christ as the son of God.

Franz Kafka said, "A book must be the axe for the frozen sea within us." For 2,000 years, Christ has been the axe for frozen hearts all over the world. His message is alive today, available to anyone who chooses to hear it.

I wrote this book to help you understand that new options are available to all of us. We aren't perfect. We all make mistakes. But our mistakes can be minimized if we take full responsibility for the choices we make.

The more choices we make for ourselves, the more likely we are to make the right choices. When we make the right choices and stay on the path of God's best for our life, our priorities and actions enter into alignment with our vision. We live life with purpose and meaning.

The Four Stones will change your life. They give you the power to overcome obstacles that other people consider insurmountable. They help you make the best choices for your life. They give you the courage to pursue your dreams no matter how insurmountable the obstacles seem.

I'm proof of that: The Exxon shift worker who never received a college degree went on to establish a multimillion-dollar corporation that became a leader in its industry.

CHAPTER 2

The Path of Default

~&~

"Insanity: doing the same thing over and over again and expecting different results."
—Albert Einstein

The two paths have existed since the beginning of time. Believe it or not, they're in the Book of Genesis. Anyone who ever spent a day in Sunday school knows that Eve was the first person to make a bad choice; Adam was the second. Adam and Eve were also the first people to choose the path of default.

There were no dangerous streams to cross in the Garden of Eden, but Eve had the opportunity to overcome an obstacle. In chapter 3 of Genesis, she faced a choice. Who would she believe: God or the serpent? She made her choice; she believed the serpent.

The serpent didn't hiss or coil itself into striking position. On the contrary, the serpent merely offered Eve a new option. She exercised her God-given power of choice when she ate the fruit that God had forbidden her to eat. Then she took some fruit to her husband.

The history of the universe changed that day. Not only because Adam and Eve ate the forbidden fruit, but because they refused to accept responsibility for what they did. Eve blamed the serpent; Adam blamed Eve. Would God have given them a second chance if they had accepted personal responsibility for their actions?

The Bible doesn't provide an answer to that question, probably because it has nothing to do with the message we're meant to learn from the story. There are only two paths in life: the path of default and the path of design. That's the message we're meant to learn.

Ever since the Garden of Eden, people have followed the path of default without realizing they were making a choice that would take them down the wrong path for the rest of their lives. As a species, we choose the wrong path over and over again and expect to build a better world. A "sane" human being is the most unnatural occurrence in all of nature. Ever since the Garden of Eden, the "natural" condition of men and women has been insanity.

The path of default is the opposite of real living. It's a path that takes us through life without a plan or a purpose, without a dream or a destination. It's a path that often leads to success—as most people define success—but never to satisfaction.

The path of default is lined with the tombstones of rich and famous people who never discovered God's purpose for their lives. From Primo Levi to the latest celebrity suicide— or "accidental overdose"—the path of default has been a highway to wealth and fame for many people who found out too late that it was a dead-end street.

Three hundred years before Christ was born, a Greek philosopher decided that our deepest desire in life is to be happy. No one in his right mind today would dispute what Aristotle said 2,300 years ago. But disagreements arise when we ask, *what makes us happy?*

There are only two paths. One is filled with travelers. It looks safe, smooth, and easy. After all, we've been taught to believe there's safety in numbers. The other path is not crowded. It looks long, hard, and dangerous. Most people go with the flow and choose the first path.

We are all masters of self-deception; we develop an ability to see only what we want to see and hear only what we want to hear. We fool ourselves all the time. The most dangerous part of living by default is that we tell ourselves we're on the right path.

One of the richest men in history left a detailed record of life on the path of default: "I observed everything going on under the sun, and really, it is all meaningless—like chasing the wind" (Ecclesiastes 1:14). The author of Ecclesiastes, King Solomon, discovered a simple truth: Money and fame make life more comfortable, but they cannot make it more satisfying.

In the last chapter of Ecclesiastes—700 wives and 300 concubines later—Solomon advises us to remember our Creator. At the end of his life, he found the answer to the question, *what makes people happy?* He discovered that true satisfaction is only possible when we follow God's path for our life.

King Solomon gave us two roadmaps: Ecclesiastes and Proverbs. For the last 3,000 years, they have shown travelers how to get on, and stay on, the right path. The story that follows is a personal experience by my friend, Jim. It's a true story about a man without a map.

The Kingdom of Default

Tim (not his real name) is insane. That's not a medical opinion: Jim is not a physician or a psychologist. But if Einstein was right, Tim is a textbook study in the nature and cause of insanity.

The Parable of the Four Stones

Tim is a king without a kingdom: He tells people he's the "King of Spain." Jim found him on the second floor of a parking building one day. Something was wrong with his leg.

"The zappers found me," he said. "This building is safe. My people cover me here."

"Who are the zappers?" Jim asked. He doesn't remember much of what he said next. In Tim's mind, the "zappers" had something to do with the same mysterious forces that were responsible for taking his throne away.

It was a hot Sunday morning in Texas. Tim was wearing a T-shirt and Bermuda shorts. His knee was badly swollen. Jim asked Tim if he had fallen, or if he had been assaulted during the night.

"The zappers found me," he repeated.

Jim's church gave Tim food, medicine, and a place to stay. One man lent him a walker. Tim was back on his feet a few days later. Not long after that, he went to a homeless shelter. When Jim spoke to Monty, the director of the shelter, he received good news: Tim was a U.S. military veteran in his sixties. He was already entitled to social security payments. The staff of the shelter was helping him with the paperwork.

"He can stay here as long as he likes," Monty said.

Three months later, Jim was surprised to see Tim sleeping outside a bus terminal. He had left the shelter before receiving his first check. Jim didn't see him for several months after that.

The next time Jim saw Tim, he was sleeping outside the same bus terminal. He showed Jim his brand-new Veterans Administration card. He had gone to the right place and had just received his first social security payment. He had no address and no bank account. The check had been mailed to a local soup kitchen. Tim had no passport, no state ID. No one would cash his check.

Jim offered to take him to his branch bank. "If you open an account," Jim explained, "Your monthly payment can be deposited directly into your account."

Tim is a likable man, a real gentleman. Jim's never met anyone quite like him. He is considerate, courteous, and good-looking. His response caught him unprepared.

"I hate banks!" he snapped. "I'll never walk into another bank as long as I live!" He had already tried to open an account; he was told he would need a state ID in addition to his VA card.

Jim was well aware of Tim's insanity by then, but fury was an emotion he hadn't seen in him before.

"Don't blame the banks," Jim said. "It's a federal law—a government requirement."

"Government!" Tim roared. "I *am* the government!"

Jim stepped back, thinking it might be wise to increase the distance between Tim's fists and his face.

"So what's the problem?" Jim said. "If you're the government, all you have to do is change the law."

Jim thought he had found a chink in Tim's armor. Maybe this was the way to help him break out of the mental cage he had built around himself.

"I am the government!" he said again. Just when Jim thought he had discovered a way to get through to Tim, the castle gate slammed shut.

The book titled '*The Kingdom of Self*' (Logos International, 1974) is written by Earl Jabay, a minister of the Reformed Church and a clinically-trained chaplain. He joined the staff of the Neuro-Psychiatric Institute in Princeton, New Jersey, in 1959.

Jabay had been trained to use treatment methods based in the behavioral sciences. He soon became frustrated by his inability to help patients at the Institute. But he was beginning to understand the cause of mental illness: His patients had descended into fantasy worlds in a last-ditch attempt to retain authority over the world around them. It is obvious Earl Jabay in *'The Kingdom of Self'* knew Tim better than all of us.

"Bit by bit, the King is forced to retreat into *un*reality, where his monarchy is unassailable," Jabay wrote. Once a diseased mind is enclosed in a fantasy world, he explained, life consists of "mentally playing out past, future and mythic events with the King always triumphantly in control."

Jim was at McDonald's the next time he saw Tim. Tim looked older; he was still living on the street. He hadn't been back to the shelter, although Monty made it clear that Tim would always be welcome there. He was carrying all his uncashed social security checks. He must have had a dozen checks in his backpack by then, but he couldn't pay for a cup of coffee.

Jim had already spoken to the New Accounts Manager at his bank. She assured him that Tim would have no trouble getting a state ID with his VA card and birth certificate (which he also carried in his backpack). She would be happy to set up his direct deposit account. When he told her about the "King-of-Spain" thing, she was professional and considerate.

At McDonald's that morning, Jim encouraged Tim to get a state ID. "You'll like the people at my bank," he said. "They can set up your account in no time. You just need a state ID."

"I'm not staying in this state long," said Tim. "I don't want to go through all the hassle of getting an ID."

Jim pointed out the obvious: Tim would need a passport or state ID to cash his checks no matter where he went. He gave it one last try.

"What's wrong with this state?" Jim asked. "We can get your ID tomorrow."

"I appreciate your concern," Tim said. He disappeared again after that.

How to Change Your Path in Life

Tim is an extreme case. How can his path in life teach us anything at all about the path of default? It teaches us more than we might think: Life by default is making the same wrong choices over and over again and expecting them to lead to happiness, fulfillment, and satisfaction.

It's easy to see that Tim is not on a path of choice. The menus at the soup kitchens are chosen for him; the hours he can relax in a public building are chosen for him too. The most important choice he makes is whether to sleep on a concrete surface or on the grass and earth. But whatever else is wrong with Tim, he still has within him the power to choose where to lay his head at night, which means he still has the power to make other choices too.

Tim chooses not to apply for a state ID. He chooses not to open a bank account. He chooses to sleep on the street instead of staying at a shelter. He exercises his power of choice every day and every night. That power is in him, and it's the only thing he needs to make a better choice the next time.

To be sure, Tim's life is an extreme example of the difference between living by design and living by default. But the difference between Tim and everyone else on the path of default isn't as big as it seems.

Most people on the path of default don't go through life pretending to be the King of Spain. But each time they let an obstacle determine the direction they take, they behave more like Tim than like the people who are already on the path of choice.

In *People-Reading: How We Control Others, How They Control Us* (Stein and Day, 1975), Ernst G. Beier and Evans

G. Valens point out a disturbing truth: Most people never take the consequences of their behavior seriously.

The message of this fascinating book is simple and profound: We are responsible for everything we do, even though most of us spend our lives looking for someone else to blame for our unhappiness.

Everything in life is a choice, whether we choose to admit it or not. The only way to change the circumstances of our life is to realize that we can consider new options and make different choices.

"The key to change," explain Beier and Valens, "lies in finding a way to break out of the walled city that constitutes our personal emotional world."

Talking to a man like Tim, we see a vivid portrait of a human mind trapped inside a walled city of its own making. We don't see the walls so clearly in the case of most people who are living life by default. But the walls are there just the same.

In *The Four Stones*, Sam Livingstone finds a way to break out of his cocoon—the "walled city" that constituted his personal emotional world up to the moment when he crossed the stream and got on the right path.

What does it take to break out of our cocoons—to soar on wings, instead of wiggling our way from nowhere to nowhere? It takes, first of all, the courage to recognize new options. That's the hardest part—the part we all need help with.

After that, the only thing it takes is something everyone already has—the power to choose.

I Can Take Care of My Own Geraniums, Thank You

Ellen J. Langer, a professor of psychology at Harvard University, is the author of *Mindfulness* (Da Capo Press, 1990), a book that examines the relationship between decision making and quality of life.

The Parable of the Four Stones

The book details the results of Langer's study of nursing home residents, which she carried out in the 1970s. Langer's work is well known. But it's worth mentioning here because of what it can tell us about the two paths.

What makes life satisfying? The results of Langer's famous study—and many other studies over the past 30 years—indicate that a person's willingness to take responsibility for his own decisions has a great deal to do with his level of satisfaction in life.

Langer divided the residents of a nursing home into two groups. People in the first group were encouraged to make more decisions about their daily lives. They could choose where to spend time with visitors, whether or not they wanted to see a movie, and when to see it. People in the second group were told that the staff of the nursing home was available to assist them whenever they needed help. They weren't encouraged to make decisions on their own.

People in both groups were given a houseplant. Residents in the first group were told that they would be responsible for taking care of the plant. Those in the second group were told that nurses would take care of the plants for them.

During the study, Langer noted that residents in the first group became more active, more energetic, and more sociable than those in the second group. When she went back to the nursing home 18 months after the study ended, she made a shocking discovery: The changed attitudes of the residents in the first group had led to a lower death rate.

A year and a half after the study ended, residents in the first group were still making more decisions for themselves than those in the second group. During the 18 months since the study ended, the death rate among residents in the second group was *twice as high* as that of the first group.

Langer's findings make perfect sense when we translate them into the language of the two paths: People who take responsibility for their own decisions—people who are on the path of choice—lead more satisfying lives than people who are on the path of default.

The path of default is a path of mindlessness. When people allow others to make decisions for them, the lifeblood is slowly sucked out of their souls. No matter how old they are when they die, the truth is that they never really lived.

Earl Jabay found a cure for mental illness. For Jabay, the solution was not a drug or a program, but a relationship with "the living God." He discovered that the only way to help his patients was to show them how to be transformed by the Spirit of God.

Every person in the world has the power to explore new options and make new choices. As every parent knows, infant children have enormous power to accept or reject a spoonful of baby food. From the earliest age, children exercise their power of choice round the clock.

All people have the power to change the path they're on. What does it take to leave the path of default and get on the path of choice? It takes courage, but not more courage than every human being already has within him. Ernst Beier and Evans Valens said it as well as anyone: "Anyone who learns that he can choose his own feelings and words and actions is a free person and a powerful person."

The Engineer designed us to make our own choices. Damage done to you by other people only diminishes your potential for happiness if you allow it to. As Eleanor Roosevelt said, "No one can make you feel inferior without your consent." No matter what you've gone through in life, you have the power to choose your own feelings and words and actions.

No one can take that power from you. It's the only power you need to get on, and stay on, the right path.

CHAPTER 3

The Path of Choice

"Never surrender your dreams. It is when we dare not live them that dreams become impossible."
—*Amazonian oral tradition*

In Part 4 of *The Four Stones*, John shows Sam the Mountains of Meaning:

> Everyone in Copyville is searching for those mountains. More people would cross the stream if they knew how near those mountains are. It doesn't take long to reach them when you're on the right path.

Sam's parents have heard about the path on the other side of the stream. "Do you remember the walks we used to take before we got married?" Sara Livingstone asks her husband. "We used to go down to the stream, near the place where Sam tried to go across. There's a path on the other side. You used to point it out to me...

"When your father died, you said the only path for you was to go to work in the mill."

Sara Livingstone has been thinking about the path she and her husband decided not to take. "Let's go down to the stream," she says. "I haven't seen the path on the other side for years."

After a day of path-walking and working at the mill, Bill Livingstone is worn out. He doesn't "feel like going anywhere."

Walking to work the next day, his thoughts wander back to the previous night's conversation. *Why do I feel like I've wasted my life? Why do I feel so unsatisfied?* For the first time in his life, he feels out of place on the path.

Sam and his mother already know why; they've been talking about John Angler while they wait for Mr. Livingstone that night. Bill is late for dinner because "something" made him stop at the stream on the way home.

When he arrives, Sara says, "The night before John left, he said something: 'God made us to be empty without him.' That's why you stopped at the stream—because you're empty and you don't know what to do about it."

Asking the Big Questions

Man's search for meaning is more than an intellectual pursuit. It arises out of our deepest need to enter into harmony with the source of all things. We live in a true "Age of Discovery." Paleontologists discover secrets of ancient history in river beds; astronomers discover exploding stars on the other side of the galaxy. But they have no answer for the simple question, *what makes people happy?*

To find lasting satisfaction in life, we need to know what we're here for. In our endless quest to unlock the secrets of the universe, we always come back to the same place in the end. Whether we're looking for answers in the heavens above or in the earth beneath our feet, we all need to answer the same question: *Why am I here?*

Our hearts are restless until we find the answer. In the absence of answers, most people live as if it were possible to be on two paths at the same time. God never intended for us to separate our lives into two different compartments: one for everything in life that's "religious" and another for everything else. But that is what we do.

The first compartment contains all the things we lump together in the "church-as-usual" category: weddings, funerals, regular church services, donations, and charitable contributions. The second compartment contains everything that doesn't belong in the first one: career, family, recreation, health and fitness, entertainment (unless it's an old Charlton Heston film). Even churchgoers describe the compartments as "sacred" and "secular."

The medieval monasteries that were designed as refuges for people who wanted to live entirely in the first compartment—people who felt called to separate themselves from the rest of society and dedicate their lives to God—are nowhere to be found in the Bible. When the apostle Paul wasn't in a Roman jail, he mingled with the crowds. He made tents for a living. His life wasn't separated into two compartments, one labeled "church" and the other "job."

Paul's tent-making wasn't something he did when he wasn't talking to people about Jesus. He always talked about Jesus. Everything he did was an expression of his purpose in life: to travel throughout the Middle East talking to people about Christ.

In our society, even people whose only exposure to "religion" is a televised Christmas concert once a year know the difference between "sacred" and "secular." Churchgoers are very much aware of the difference between Sunday and the rest of the week. We try to keep one foot on the other path as we walk down our chosen path. We tell ourselves that we're maintaining a healthy balance by making room for both compartments in our lives, though we sense at times that our souls are coming apart at the seams.

We think about God for an hour or two on Sunday, if we think about him at all. We don't notice God's fingerprints on the people and things around us as we go through the rest of the week. We put God in a box and let him out for an hour or two on Sunday, while following a path of our own making the rest of the time. We base our choices on what's happening in the economy, on what our friends and relatives think we should do, or on what a business partner or customer thinks is right. In short, we base our decisions on just about anything except what the Bible says.

We live on a path of "logical choices" from Monday to Saturday, while clinging to the illusion that we can jump off the regular path and land on the "life-with-purpose" path in time for a Sunday morning church service. Our vision suffers as a result. Not our "eyesight," of course, but the kind of vision that gives meaning to life.

When a society separates life into compartments, as ours does, most people go through life with the idea that success contains a large element of luck. Rich and successful people got a "lucky break" that we missed out on. Maybe they were just born with more talent than the rest of us.

The real tragedy of compartmentalized living is that most people never realize they don't have to make major life decisions alone. A century of vocational training and emphasis on college career tracks has produced a society that relies on job-market forecasts and other economic indicators to make decisions about the direction we take in life.

Do you know what you're here for? Have you discovered your purpose in life? Do you have a clear vision of where you want to be ten years from now?

As far as I remember, I never heard a teacher ask these questions in a classroom, not even at the college level. It's no wonder people go through midlife crises in a society that sends young people into the world without a purpose to live for.

Conflicts arise in our personal lives due to the way we answer the question, *what is the purpose of my life?* Whether your answer is conscious or unconscious, every turn and twist in your life is based on how you respond to that question. If you don't provide your own answer, someone or something else will determine your direction in life.

The foundation of a satisfying marriage must be laid long before the wedding ceremony begins. Your marriage won't be satisfying if you aren't sure of your future spouse's answers to the questions: *Do you have a vision for your life? Do we have a vision for our life together?* A satisfying marriage, one in which two people stay happy together past the first stretch of stormy weather, must be based on a shared vision for the future.

People don't stay the same, even when there appears to be no change in their lives over a period of decades. Change is a constant in everything that's alive. And the fundamental change in a human life is this: At any point in life, a person is either moving closer to God or farther from him.

My wife and I learned this lesson when we made a choice to relocate.

A Time to Choose

In 2002 Kim and I decided to purchase a plot of land in Friendswood, Texas, a suburb of Houston. The tall trees and gated community convinced us that it was the perfect place to build our dream home.

When we decided later that year to invest more in our business, we put the plans for our dream home on hold. In 2003 we began the remodel of our existing home in Pearland, Texas, a few miles from Friendswood. The remodeling project made our old house more livable but it took its toll on us in time, money and stress. With the pressures of a growing business and exhausted from an extended remodeling project we realized we would have to wait a little longer to build on our new land.

All that changed in 2006 when we decided to sell the business. My wife was the Chief Financial Officer. I was President and Chief Executive Officer. We hadn't planned to sell; we were forced out of our positions as CFO and CEO by our Board of Directors. I had a lucrative contract as President and CEO of a leading analytical instrumentation company in the U.S. Although I can't divulge the specifics, I had an employment contract and I had refused to release the contract. Our organization was in an expansion mode and my contract would have been worth even more money on the back side of the expansion. We didn't do anything wrong; it was simply a business decision for them to buy out my contract than to pay me what it was worth after the merger.

Selling the business created new options for us. We could stay in the Houston area or relocate anywhere we wanted. We decided to take a driving vacation in the western United States, a trip we had dreamed of making for many years. We used to enjoy driving vacations but in the years of running a business we never had the time. Now we did.

Kim and I visited 13 states on the month-long trip. We had a lot of time to talk, to plan, and to dream. I thought I wanted to take on another executive job; Kim believed God was leading us in a different direction. Before the trip was over, we decided to move to a new area: McKinney, Texas, about 30 miles north of Dallas. We felt drawn to a church there: Celebration Covenant Church (CCC). Kim and I believed that God's path for our lives was leading us to CCC.

CCC is a ministry based on the concept of "church should be the most creative place in the universe" and "servant leadership." Before our trip, God had told Kim, "You won't do church as usual any longer." CCC was a place where we would be able to make a contribution through our desire to serve and our experience as business leaders. We believed that the opportunity to get actively involved in ministry at CCC would stimulate our spiritual growth more than if we stayed in Houston or became more involved at our current church which we loved.

We left our newly remodeled home in Pearland and our undeveloped plot of land in Friendswood to relocate five hours away, all because we knew God was leading us to a new church.

Kim and I had a burning in our hearts to grow in God in an unusual way. We felt the same desire in the people we knew at CCC. Our young grandchildren were also in the McKinney area: We wanted to watch them grow more than we cared about our high-paying jobs in corporate America. We knew our decision to relocate was part of God's plan for our life.

We based our decision not on what seemed best from a business standpoint, but on our best understanding of God's path for our lives. From a business perspective, I thought selling the business was a mistake, but I had left myself no choice in the matter.

In 2000 I sold 51% of the company I founded, Peak Analytical Inc., to form an international partnership with a company headquartered in Switzerland. At the time, I thought the new partnership was in the best interest of my company and my employees. Looking back, I could easily regret my decision six years later when Kim and I were forced out. It would be easy to blame my partners but it truly isn't their fault. I firmly believe God orchestrated my exit to position me to further grow into the next level of my purpose. I still honor my time and friendships from that period in my life.

Leaving the Houston area wasn't a popular decision. It wasn't a sensible choice from the point of view of the people around us. Literally everyone we knew was against our decision to relocate.

Everyone thought we had "gone over the deep end." We paid cash for a new house in McKinney before we sold our old home in Pearland and the plot of land in Friendswood. Although we left everything behind, Kim and I never doubted that we were following the path of God's best for our life. We were totally clear: We made a decision to trust God.

I know today it had to be God's plan, or I wouldn't have been so clear about moving before we sold our house. The way our lives have gone since moving to McKinney proves to us that we made the right choice—a choice based entirely on where we thought God wanted us to be in the future.

Following the path of God's purpose isn't always popular with family and friends. People said things like: "You're leaving the church you love." "You're leaving your friends." "All your customers know you; they'll support you in a new business here." "You're leaving your son and your daughter-in-law." "You should wait until your home and land sell before moving." "You're leaving your elderly father alone." My mother had just died so there were considerable emotional ties to stay. Many people thought we were just running away – and we were – running to stay on God's path of purpose for our lives.

We didn't have answers for all these objections. But following God's path instead of the path that makes logical sense is always beneficial and rewarding. It isn't always an easy path. It requires us to learn new things. Sometimes we must start over without a business or a job.

Learning to follow God's path has forced me to recognize that my ways aren't always right. I had to learn to see myself from God's point of view: I had to elevate my thinking to elevate my life, which allows me to elevate the life of those around me. I had to understand the difference between "servant leaders" and volunteers. Servant leaders lead themselves to "act their way into a feeling." Volunteers

The Parable of the Four Stones

have to "feel their way into an action." Volunteers won't act if they don't feel like it.

Relocating to McKinney began a new stage in our lives by giving us the opportunity to build a closer relationship with God. My level of commitment and my level of giving increased. I no longer focused my energy on business success; my new focus was on "something bigger than myself." Serving others became the purpose of my life. My wife became more important to me as we built a new relationship based on God and each other instead of on the business interests we used to have in common.

Following the path of God's purpose for our lives has strengthened our marriage and given each of us the opportunity to grow as an individual. It would have been easy to find excuses not to relocate. We had recently purchased our "dream land" and remodeled our house. Staying in the Houston area would have been the logical thing to do.

Thanks to the choice we made, Kim and I discovered this simple secret: When God gives us a vision of his path for our lives, we can be sure it leads to our "Peak of Satisfaction."

In the Beginning

In Part 2 of *The Four Stones*, John teaches Sam how to discover "God's fingerprints."

"An ordinary birch tree, one you've walked by every day in your life, can reveal a piece of God's plan," he says.

John shows Sam a cocoon. "Until today," he explains, "you were in the caterpillar stage. Now you're in a cocoon. You're turning into a new person."

Sam is beginning to understand: No one is meant to be in Copyville forever.

The Four Stones is a model of God's creative process. Like every model, it represents something larger than itself:

God's process for bringing things into existence. The Creation vs. Evolution debate will probably never be settled in a way that satisfies 100% of the scientists in the world. Speaking as a Christian and a chemist, I believe God created the universe and everything in it exactly as the Book of Genesis reveals.

From a spiritual perspective, my Christian faith is all I need to believe that Genesis is literally true. From a scientific perspective, I need only two words to settle the debate in my own mind: Intelligent Design. As a Christian and a chemist, I think it's absurd to believe that a system as complex as the human eye—or as powerful and precise as the eye of an eagle—could have come into existence without vision, planning, balance, and action on the part of a Designer.

The first chapter in the Bible teaches us a great deal about God's creativity. Everything God created in Genesis was the result of vision, plan, balance, and action. The opening verses of the Bible give us a clear picture of how God used *The Four Stones* to create everything that exists:

- After God created the heavens and the earth, "The earth was formless and empty, and darkness covered the deep waters. And the Spirit of God was hovering over the surface of the waters" (Genesis 1:2).
- The *vision* and *plan* already existed in God's mind as his Spirit moved over the earth.
- God took *action*: "Then God said, 'Let there be light,' and there was light" (v. 3).
- "Then he separated the light from the darkness." God achieved *balance* by creating day and night (v. 4-5).

The Four Stones is not only a model of God's creative process. It's a system every person in the world can use, here and now, to bring desired outcomes into existence. God gave us the first chapter of Genesis to show us *The Four Stones* in action. They are available to every person alive today.

The Four Stones are God-given tools that will change the circumstances of your life when you put them in action, even as they bring about deep, lasting change in the person you are. When you use *The Four Stones* to shape the future, God makes you a new person by changing the way you think. Using God's tools to transform your world transforms your own mind in the process.

When we implement *The Four Stones* in our lives, we bring ourselves into alignment with God's system for bringing about desired outcomes. *The Four Stones* existed in God's mind before the creation of the universe. I stumbled onto the system, awkwardly and haphazardly at first. I lost my footing a time or two and fell smack into my obstacle. But God designed us in such a way that we cannot fail to discover his best path for our life if we let him guide us.

The only thing that can prevent you from discovering the path of God's best is your own resistance or refusal to believe that it exists. Harriet Beecher Stowe wrote, "When you get into a tight place and everything goes against you, till it seems as though you could not hang on a minute longer, never give up then, for that is just the place and time that the tide will turn."

As long as you keep using *The Four Stones*—and as long as you don't give up—your success is guaranteed by the Tide-Turner himself.

One Small Step

Hundreds of years before the birth of Christ, the prophet Jeremiah received a guarantee directly from God. It came in the form of a lesson much like the one John Angler gave Sam in Part 2 of *The Four Stones*. When God first spoke to Jeremiah, he gave the prophet a vision:

Then the LORD said to me, "Look, Jeremiah! What do you see?" And I replied, "I see a branch from an almond tree." And the LORD said, "That's right, and it means that I am watching, and I will certainly carry out all my plans" (Jeremiah 1:11-12).

God promises to carry out his plans. What would your life be like if you had a guarantee from God that you couldn't fail? If your projects and goals are the ones God planned for your life, you already have that guarantee.

That doesn't mean you'll never suffer setbacks; it doesn't mean you'll never lose a battle. It means that as long as your dreams come from God, and as long as you don't give up on your dreams, God will make a way for you to accomplish them.

The Book of Job tells the story of a man who heard about God from others all his life. One day he saw God with his own eyes. When that happened, his doubts, fears, and uncertainties melted away. We can't know God until we get on his path. Our fears, doubts, and uncertainties stay with us because most of us have only heard about God from others.

When Jeremiah learned that God had chosen him to be a "prophet to the nations," he replied, "O Sovereign LORD, I can't speak for you! I'm too young!" (Jeremiah 1:6)

God told Jeremiah not to be afraid, "for I will be with you and will protect you" (v. 8).

We don't set goals because we're afraid of failing. We all fail sometimes. So what? If my wife and I hadn't been forced out of our positions at our company, we wouldn't be where we are today. When you're on the path of God's best for your life, even failure happens at the right time and place.

If you keep doing what you've always done, you'll get the same results you've always had in life. Change depends on the ability to explore new options and to make new choices. Establish a goal today knowing that you *can't fail to accomplish it.* Write it in your Bible. If you don't have a Bible, write it in this book.

The reason people don't set goals is lack of faith—lack of faith in themselves and lack of faith in God.

Ask yourself: *What goal would I set if the Creator of the universe guaranteed my success?* This is the first step to discovering your God-given purpose in life.

You'll learn more about how to discover God's vision for your life in the next chapter. For now, write down one goal you would choose if you had a guarantee directly from God that you couldn't fail. Go ahead; stop reading and write down your one goal.

Jesus said, "Anyone who wants to do the will of God will know whether my teaching is from God or is merely my own" (John 7:17).

We can't discover the answer to the Big Questions until we have the clarity of vision that only comes when we learn to see ourselves from God's point of view. If you haven't discovered God's purpose for your life, make it your number one priority today.

"When you start spinning out all kinds of different solutions, you're on the road to total chaos," says author Jack Trout. "Simplicity requires that you narrow the options and return to a single path."

As a society, we need to pay serious attention to Trout's advice. As individuals, there is something we can do about the road to total chaos that world leaders seem bent on following: We can choose to follow God's path. God promises to restore our land if we seek his guidance through worship and prayer (2 Chronicles 7:14).

If God created you for the purpose of teaching leaders how to narrow their options and return to a single path, you've gotten off to a good start by reading this book. No matter what God has planned for your life, one small step is all it takes to get on the right path.

CHAPTER 4

Vision

*"Vision is the ability to see God's presence,
to perceive God's power, to focus on God's plan
in spite of the obstacles."*
—Charles Swindoll

In Part 3 of *The Four Stones*, Sam writes his answers to the Big Questions. If published reports are accurate, only three of every 100 persons take the time to do what Sam did. The other 97 live and die without having written down an answer to the question, *what am I here for?*

Let's take a closer look at Sam's vision statement:

> Tell people about the two paths. Show them the 4 stones and teach them how to cross the stream (like John taught me). A big part of this is helping people understand that Jesus makes your life more satisfying. You will accomplish more with Jesus in your life than without him!

Reflecting on what he has just written, Sam adds:

To accomplish my vision, I need to change the way I think (in other words, I have to break out of my cocoon, because as long as I'm in it, it's a case of the blind leading the blind). I need to get on (and stay on) my right path. To get on the right path I need to make RIGHT CHOICES.

It isn't hard to imagine what might have happened after the end of *The Four Stones*. At some point on his journey back to Copyville, Sam probably wrote a more focused statement of his purpose in life. Sam's vision can be expressed in one sentence:

To help people achieve satisfaction in life by getting on, and staying on, God's path.

Life on a Different Level

Sam's conversation with John at the stream gave him a clear picture of God's vision for his life. It takes most people years to reach this point, if they reach it at all.

Vision is as important for companies, organizations, and countries as it is for individuals. Every successful business person knows that companies flounder when they don't have a clear vision of where they want to go. Lack of vision explains why more than half of all small business startups fail in the first three years.

A vision tells you—or your organization—where to go and how to get there. But it's much more than just a goal or a destination you want to reach. We all know people who have one goal today, only to exchange it for a different goal the first time they run into an obstacle. True vision gives people the power to overcome obstacles.

The most important thing the Bible teaches about vision is this: *Vision isn't natural.* The natural condition of humanity is to plod through life with no higher purpose than to get through another week, another month, or another year. Most people simply endure life. Look at the people around you and you'll see what I mean. Living without a vision is the most natural way to live.

According to the Bible, the same power that God used to raise Jesus from the dead lives in people today when they are filled with God's spirit. This is the only power in the universe that can cure mental illness, as Earl Jabay discovered at the Neuro-Psychiatric Institute in Princeton. It's the only power that can rescue people like Tim from the "walled city" they live in. It's the only power that can help you overcome obstacles and keep you moving forward on the path of God's best for your life.

True vision is *supernatural* because it comes from God, a supernatural being. It isn't "natural" for people to have a vision at all, which explains why 97 of every 100 people in the world go through life without a vision. When a vision comes from God, who is a supernatural being, it fills our life with his Spirit, which gives us the wisdom and power to face and overcome obstacles.

"When we look at life with vision," says Charles Swindoll, "we perceive events and circumstances with God's thoughts." (Charles Swindoll, *Living Above the Level of Mediocrity*, Word Books, 1987). When we discover God's vision for our lives, our doubts and fears melt away. The obstacles we face don't look so big when we know we were born to accomplish a vision.

The Bible is a guidebook for people who want to live life by design. As we read the Bible, we begin to realize that we're hearing the same message over and over again. It's the story of ordinary men and women—people that were afraid to break out of their "cocoons" at first—who did extraordinary things once they realized that God was their guide.

Business analysts agree on one fundamental point: Lack of vision is the main cause of failure in business. The terminology differs from one analyst to the next. But whether people talk about core businesses, corporate missions, purpose statements, or organizational visions, the lesson is the same: Organizations perish when they don't have a clear vision for the future.

This is the first lesson Sam learns in *The Four Stones*: We can't overcome obstacles without a clear vision of what we want to accomplish on the other side of the problem. That's the "problem" with problems: A problem disrupts our peace of mind by forcing us to do something in a different way.

Problems don't just demand our attention: They remind us of the need to find a better way to do something. Problems are frustrating and stressful because we see them as interruptions in our otherwise comfortable routines.

When we understand that God allows problems and obstacles because without them we become too comfortable on a level of existence far below what we ought to be, we start to see our problems in a different light. The Bible is the story of how God nudges people out of their "comfort zones" to achieve a vision that's always much larger than their own personal worlds. Our comfort zones are not the places to find lasting satisfaction anyway. If they were, most people would already be satisfied.

We only need to watch toddlers for a few moments to remind ourselves of this simple truth. Surrounded by strangers in a public place, the safest and most comfortable zone for small children would seem to be as close to their parents as they can get. But children dash away from their parents' side at the first opportunity.

We weren't created to stay in the same place for long. Children know this instinctively. Success and satisfaction come to those adults that retain a childlike need to keep moving, to keep exploring new options, and to keep expanding their horizons.

When Jesus told his disciples that to enter the kingdom of heaven they had to become like little children, he was referring to the fearlessness of children as much as to their innocence. Jesus reminded his disciples of a profound truth: Small children aren't afraid to change the path they're on.

"My ways are higher than your ways and my thoughts higher than your thoughts," God told the prophet Isaiah.

What's the difference between God's thoughts and our thoughts? As God told Jeremiah, he carries out his plans. Obstacles don't change God's vision. When we run into obstacles, a vision of God's purpose for our life keeps us focused on the right path. When we have a vision, we aren't pushed off our path by the first obstacle we encounter.

A vision brings our thoughts into alignment with God's thoughts. Nothing is impossible for men and women with a vision. Visionary leaders aren't afraid of the unknown. When business leaders have a vision of where they want their companies to go, they don't worry about economic forecasts.

People who are guided by a vision begin to realize that economic recessions and strong competitors aren't the real enemies: The only obstacle that can defeat us is our own worry and fear. A true vision is bigger than all our worries and uncertainties. When we get on God's path for our life, we begin to understand, bit by bit and day by day, that a vision from God is the antidote for fear and doubt.

One Idea from God Will Change Your Life

How can you be sure a vision is from God? How can you be sure you're following God's path? When you're on God's path, doors of opportunity open that no man can open; doors close that no man can close. I found that out when I built a multimillion-dollar company based on one idea.

The idea was to have an analytical laboratory that offered one specialized service and that would be the best in the world at what it did. The vision came to me when I was working for Dionex Corporation, a leader in the field of ion analysis. My job at Dionex gave me an up-close look at how poorly most labs ran their instruments and service business. I realized that the quality of the analysis they delivered left a lot of room for improvement.

I received the training I needed to excel in such a highly technical business when I was at Exxon. I had been the coordinator of Exxon's distillation lab in Baytown when I moved to the Research Center. I became responsible for a new technology called "Ion Chromatography." I worked for a Ph.D. at Exxon, Dr. Kishore Nadkarni, who encouraged me to explore the possibilities of this new analytical process.

Ion Chromatography is an analytical instrumentation technique for analyzing ions in such matrices as water. Ion Chromatography measures ions using a separations process; for example: Chloride in drinking water; Phosphates in soft drinks; Amines in nuclear reactor water and so forth.

At Exxon I developed the analytical process for measuring anions in coal after an ignition process. I flourished as a researcher in the innovative environment at Exxon. I discovered new ways to use Ion Chromatography and wrote technical papers to present the results of my research.

Exxon wanted me to move to Baton Rouge, Louisiana. My wife and I wanted to stay in Houston. In 1984 I left Exxon to go to work for Dionex.

My first job at Dionex was in customer service. Flying all over the country as a customer service representative, I soon realized that my job wasn't going to let me see my children grow up. After a few years I requested and received a transfer from customer service to sales.

The Parable of the Four Stones

In my new position, I was selling Dionex instruments and software to customers in Texas and Louisiana. Customers in my sales territory asked me to provide the level of support I used to provide when I was in customer service. That's when the idea to launch my own company came to me.

In my "Big Vision," I pictured myself in a room filled with state-of-the-art computer controlled instrumentation, rolling in my chair from one instrument to another. I was working over 60 hours a week, driving across half the state of Texas as a sales representative for Dionex.

When will I have time to start a laboratory? I thought to myself. I didn't have enough money to dream about purchasing the expensive instrumentation I needed to start my own company.

Though I continued to be diligent in my sales job at Dionex, I knew the time had come to step onto my first stone. As I went about my day job, I envisioned myself working in my own lab and doing customer service in the field as an add-on to the business. I wrote down "The Vision," just like Sam did in *The Four Stones*.

I wrote "The Plan" down next: small steps which I believed were attainable. I knew I would be able to measure my progress by checking off one step after another as I accomplished small goals. To achieve The Vision and The Plan, I knew I was going to need Balance in my life, especially in the financial areas.

These three areas were coming into clear focus, but I hadn't taken Action yet. I continued to take care of my customers at Dionex as I prepared to step onto my Action stone. Then an amazing thing happened: I was offered an Ion Chromatography instrument for pennies on the dollar. The offer was made to me by a government-sponsored biotech firm that had lost its funding. The government was forcing the firm to sell the instrument.

The Parable of the Four Stones

"Do you know anyone who would be interested?" I was asked.

The firm had no way to know I wanted one. I borrowed the money from my father, which allowed me to accomplish one of the first steps of my plan. Then another amazing thing happened: I was offered two more of these instruments by a firm that had been one of my customers. I bought them for even less than pennies on the dollar.

The final piece of my plan fell into place when one of my customers asked me to join his company. When I declined his invitation, he offered me the use of a room at his environmental lab to set up my instruments in. I left my job at Dionex one week later.

The Vision and The Plan were in Balance. I took Action and never looked back.

The new company, Peak Analytical Inc., was launched in 1991. My wife and I were living in Pearland, Texas. Our children were still at home, which made me extremely conscious of the risk I was taking in starting a new company from scratch. Word of mouth was mostly responsible for the rapid growth of the new company: Good work in this industry gets talked about at conferences and other forums.

I eventually had 32 Ion Chromatographs and two Capillary Electrophoresis instruments in my fully automated lab. I hired chemists to help operate the equipment because of all the business. Many new clients called on the company because we were the best at what we did.

Over the next 15 years, I lived The Vision. I followed The Plan and took Action. I modified the Plan frequently to maintain my Balance. I took Action to keep moving forward on the path of God's purpose for my life. I took the company from a small "mom-and-pop" business to a large international firm. After making millions of dollars for Peak Analytical during these first few years as President and CEO, I sold the company in April of 2000.

It all started with a decision to discover God's path for my life instead of doing what others thought I should do. Adult males in the Brewer family went to work in the local refineries. I was expected to follow in their footsteps. By stepping into God's vision for my life, I acquired the passion, power, and wisdom to make my dream come true.

Each time I overcome an obstacle instead of letting the obstacle push me onto a different path, I have proof that *The Four Stones* are real. No matter what the obstacle looks like, the path of God's best is always waiting for me on the other side.

It seems natural when obstacles force people to change their direction in life. But each time we let circumstances determine the course we take, we act more like caterpillars than like the creatures God created us to be.

Writing Your Vision

Discovering a vision for your life is the first step toward becoming who you ought to be. Writing your vision down is the first step toward living it. The goal you chose in the last chapter will tell you a lot about God's purpose for your life. If you weren't sure before, you probably have a clearer sense of your vision after reading this chapter.

Ask God to help you understand his purpose for your life. If you don't have a clear vision right away, don't give up. The answer usually comes when you're least expecting it:

1. Write your major goal at the top of a 3x5 card. Below your major goal, write as many things as you can think of that will happen after you accomplish it. This is all part of your vision.

2. Picture the life you want to be living ten years from now. Write a description of it. A vision of where you want to be in the future will help you know how to handle situations today. A vision for the future tells you the things you need to do—and the traps you must avoid—to move closer to your goal. As Brian Tracy says, "If what you are doing is not moving you towards your goals, then it's moving you away from your goals."

What you write today might not be a specific vision of God's purpose for your life, but it's a crucial first step toward discovering your purpose. Don't let yourself feel frustrated if you don't have a clear vision for your life right away. Keep working at it until you start to form a mental picture of the person you're meant to become.

If you don't feel passionate about a goal, it will never lead to the path of God's best for your life. If you aren't passionate about something, you'll feel empty no matter how successful you become. Always ask yourself why you want to achieve a goal: To increase your self-esteem? To impress others? To be rich? These things are all results of success. But if they're the only motives that drive you, success will bring no satisfaction when you achieve it.

God's vision for your life will always be something that creates benefits for others. Business owners tend to look *inward*—on the products and services they offer. They typically have a vision that focuses on the business itself. God's vision for your business will always challenge you to focus *outward*—on the people you serve. As Albert Einstein said, "Only a life lived for others is a life worth while."

One sentence on a 3x5 card can change your life. If you don't write it down, you'll be less committed to doing something about it. What you write today may not be the same vision you have when you finish this book. Discovering a

The Parable of the Four Stones

vision for your life is usually a process rather than a one-time event. The important thing today is to take another small step in the right direction.

It is my hope that you'll be ready to write your personal vision statement by the time you finish this book. That alone will put you in an elite category: The three out of every 100 people in the world who know where they're going.

CHAPTER 5

Plan

༄

*"Goals are dreams we convert to plans
and take action to fulfill."*
—Zig Ziglar

When we discover God's purpose for our life, we have a clear vision of where we want to go. The next thing we need is a plan to guide us toward our goal, one step at a time.

Before we step onto the Stone of Plan, we need to check our bearings. We need to be sure we're moving in the right direction, and we need a clear understanding of what we've learned so far.

Words like *vision*, *mission*, and *purpose* are used in organizations of all shapes and sizes, from Fortune 500 companies to the "mom-and-pop" business down the street. I'm sure many people are confused by the way these terms are used in business.

When business people talk about vision, mission, and purpose, do they mean the same thing? Are they talking about three different things? The simple answer to both questions is "yes." Some people use the terms interchangeably, while others insist on making a distinction.

For the purposes of my topic—getting on, and staying on, God's path for your life—I have chosen to use the terms interchangeably. People can split hairs over this if they like, but it doesn't matter as far as satisfaction in life is concerned.

I've made a choice to follow Jack Trout's advice—to "narrow the options and return to a single path." In the interest of simplicity, *vision, mission*, and *purpose* mean the same thing in my book: where you want to go, why you want to go there, and what you want the future to be like.

No matter what you call it, success and satisfaction come to people who answer these questions.

Can I Change Myself?

"A book must be the axe for the frozen sea within us," Kafka said. He wasn't a religious man, but few people have seen into the human heart as clearly as he did. What he saw was a "frozen sea," which was Kafka's name for the "walled city" that Ernst Beier and Evans Valens wrote about in their book.

Kafka was right about one thing: If a book doesn't change the way we think, it isn't worth our time. Nothing can satisfy us in life until we discover "the axe for the frozen sea within," to which author Wendy Kaminer adds, "Self-help is how we skate."

The Four Stones is a story about a place where people skate through life: Their hearts are frozen. They remain unaware of the possibilities that life offers. Compared with what they ought to be, they are only half awake. The story doesn't tell us, but I wouldn't be surprised if self-help books were bestsellers in Copyville too.

Look at any list of bestsellers and you'll see the same well-worn themes at the top of every list. The titles change from month to month and year to year, but the main theme remains the same. On every list, you'll find at least one or two "How-To-Be-Happy-And-Successful" books.

Year after year, the Gallup Poll tells us that the majority of Americans are "satisfied with the way their lives are going." If most people are satisfied with their lives, why are they spending money on books that promise to teach them how to be happier and more successful?

What's going on? Maybe people aren't telling Gallup the truth. Maybe they're hiding the truth from themselves.

Most adults have never taken the time to plan their lives. Like Bill Livingstone, they rarely question their path in life. We might not say so when the Gallup people ask, but most of us secretly admit, at least once in our lives, that our dreams haven't come true.

Denis Waitley explains what went wrong: "The reason most people never reach their goals is that they don't define them, or ever seriously consider them as believable or achievable."

In Part 2 of *The Four Stones*, Sam wants to cross the stream with John. "Take me with you," he says. But Sam needs to learn one more thing.

"You won't be ready to leave Copyville until you learn how to lead yourself," says John.

Sam learns many valuable lessons at the stream that day. The most valuable lesson of all is the last one: "You're leading yourself when you act your way into a feeling instead of feeling your way into an action."

Sam thinks about John's words the rest of the day. Thanks to a wise mentor, Sam is beginning to understand what wise men and women have understood since King Solomon's day: Whether we know it or not, we have chosen to be what we are.

Sam learns—how could he forget?—that the key to every good plan is SAM: Specific, Attainable, Measurable steps. He writes down his "SAM" steps in the "Plan" section of his purpose statement.

Sam's "SAM" contains all the elements of a quality plan:

- It's **Specific**: Sam's plan is a detailed roadmap of the steps he needs to take to accomplish his vision. His list includes seven specific action steps.
- It's **Attainable**: John told Sam that he only needed to learn one more thing before he was ready to cross the stream. John could be trusted as a mentor: He led his own daughter across the stream. When Angela Angler crossed, she was no older than Sam was when he fell into the stream.
- It's **Measurable**: Like every winning plan, Sam's Plan includes a system for measuring his progress.

I'm leading myself when I see a vision for my life; when I write it down as clearly as I can; when I set timelines for everything I want to do; when I set goals and plan how I'm going to reach them; when I remember to use the 4 stones every time I run into an obstacle (and when I don't run into obstacles, because I need the 4 stones all the time).

Sam is ready to pursue his dream. He sets a timeline for putting his plan into motion: *As Soon As Possible!* In a "Post Script" he adds, "I'm ready to go because I wrote this down. That means I'm learning how to lead myself."

Sam is checking his roadmap and measuring his progress. He's learning how to put "SAM" to work in his life.

As Sam writes draft after draft of his purpose statement, in the back of his mind is the question that philosophers have asked since the beginning of time: *Can I change myself?*

The Parable of the Four Stones

Most people would rather not know the answer. It's easier to blame "circumstances" and "unlucky breaks" for what we have become. People in Copyville don't ask the question—they can't face that much responsibility.

Sam sees the truth that Ernst Beier discovered in his career: "Anyone who learns that he can choose his own feelings and words and actions is a free person and a powerful person."

Sam is ready to take responsibility for the choices he makes. He has a clear vision of what he wants the future to be like. He has a plan for accomplishing his vision.

In Part 4 of *The Four Stones*, we learn that "Sam's plan went without a hitch." He crosses the stream and gets on God's path for his life. But first Sam must take care of some unfinished business with Dick Defiant and Steve Sullen, the boys that saved his life.

Dick and Steve dared Sam to cross the stream the day he almost drowned. They were as much to blame for the near disaster as Sam was. Terrified of what their parents might do when they learned the truth, Dick and Steve invented a story that the townspeople swallowed "lock, stock, and barrel." Their falsified version branded Sam as a "potential troublemaker" in the eyes of the townspeople. Sam never told the true story to anyone, not even to his parents. He closed himself inside a walled city.

Standing on the front porch of Steve Sullen's house, Sam is a free person and a powerful person. The first purpose of his visit is to thank Dick and Steve for saving his life. "I should have done it a long time ago," he says.

Sam breaks out of the walled city: His conversation with Dick and Steve is proof of his transformation. He has taken responsibility for changing the way he thinks so that God can make him a new person.

Can I change myself? "Not easily, and perhaps not at all," wrote Ernst Beier. Beier believed that "self-control" is seldom effective. To put it another way, self-help barely scratches the surface of the frozen sea within us, as Wendy Kaminer would say.

Ernst Beier concluded that people only change when an "unexpected response" motivates them "to make them change themselves." Beier wrote from the point of view of a secular psychologist, but his conclusions "reveal a piece of God's plan," to put it in John Angler's words.

Sam is the "unexpected response" in the lives of four other people. "If everything goes according to plan," he tells John the night before he returns to Copyville, "four people will break out of their cocoons tomorrow. I don't want to miss it."

Sam is talking about Dick, Steve, and his parents. He can't control what these four persons decide to do, of course. But Sam's enthusiasm leads us to believe that all four will soon be ready to break out of their own walled cities.

What motivates Sam to want to change himself? Sam's transformation is triggered by the most powerful "unexpected response" in the history of mankind: the Spirit of God, which motivates people all over the world to want to change themselves.

"We don't engineer the change, but we have a part to play in the process," John explained. This is the mystery that fills Sam's thoughts as the story ends—the question he wants to be sure to ask the next time he sees John.

Sam is "new to the Book." But he has already taken a huge step forward on the path of God's best: He has learned to take responsibility for his own feelings and words and actions.

Alignment Before Assignment

Two years ago, I learned how important it is to bring our plans into alignment with God's purpose for our life.

The Parable of the Four Stones

Kim and I had just left our company. The 30-day driving vacation we took in the western United States wasn't just a vacation: I had an interview for a high-profile executive position in the San Francisco Bay Area. The interview was only a formality. The job was mine if I wanted it.

Kim and I spent the night before the interview in Carmel By The Sea. When I got up that morning, I said to Kim, "I can't accept this job. We have to move to McKinney to attend Celebration Covenant Church."

Kim had a big smile on her face. "I was wondering how long it would take for you to hear God," she said.

I called and declined the position.

The choice I made that morning in California brought my plan into alignment with God's purpose for my life. But my favorite illustration of successful planning is a story that unfolded much closer to home.

My daughter, Jessica, was a high-spirited, curly-haired youth who dreamed of being an athlete. She started school a year early because of her intelligence. From an early age she could hold her own with most adults in any type of conversation. She was a year younger than her classmates, which put her at a disadvantage in sports.

She was the smallest girl that tried out for the freshman volleyball team in high school. At that level, coaches expected players to have the height and jumping ability to reach the top of the net. Coaches discouraged players from using the underhand serve that Jessica had turned into one of her best weapons on the court. Players in high school were expected to use an overhand serve, or they didn't serve at all.

As tryouts began, Jessica seemed too short to make the cut. But her mind was made up: She wouldn't take "no" for an answer. Jessica's passion and desire caught the eye of the coaches, who saw a level of energy and passion in her that was missing in some of the more physically gifted players.

Although she made the team, it was a year of physical struggles for her. She put forth her best effort every day and began to earn playing time in games. She practiced hard and played hard.

The coaches saw improvement in her technique and understanding of the game, but Jessica's size kept her from getting an opportunity to play more. Her mother and I encouraged her to pursue her talent for music. She did—but she stayed on the volleyball team too.

As the season progressed, Jessica was given a little playing time on the back row, where all she had to do was pass the ball to other players. She hadn't served in a game all season long. In a game near the end of her freshman season, the coach put Jessica in to serve.

Jessica took her stance behind the back line, got set, and made a perfect overhand serve. For a second or two, Kim and I were breathless as we watched the ball float over the top of the net and drop into the opponent's court untouched.

Amazing! Everyone stood and cheered, even the coach. Jessica had carried out her mission to perfection. The expression on my daughter's face told me what I already knew in my heart: One winning serve made all the hard work and sacrifice worth it.

Jessica's Plan Pays Off

In the off season, Jessica played club volleyball and worked on her game. She had a tough coach, Doug McGown, who had already coached a team that won the state championship. Coach McGown was hard on Jessica, but he appreciated her desire. He taught her as much about life as he taught her about volleyball that season.

When Jessica went back to Pearland High School, her coaches realized that she had improved more than her teammates during the summer vacation. She was selected to play the setter position, where she became known for her precision passing and uncanny ability to save balls. Moving around the court flawlessly, Jessica made the game look easy. Her team had a great year.

During the rest of her high school career Jessica played a part in many victories, thanks to her skill as a setter and a server. She served several complete games, keeping opponents off balance with her ability to move the ball around the court. Her overhand serve was a perfect blend of power, accuracy, and unpredictability. As a setter, she could put the ball in perfect position for her teammates to pound over the net.

Jessica discovered that her compact body, which had been a disadvantage at first, could be turned into an advantage. She was known for scooping up low balls before they hit the court, chasing down and saving errant passes, and setting the ball back across the court to her waiting hitters.

Jessica accomplished more in her high school career than many of her teammates who were more physically gifted. She made a decision: Nothing was going to stop her from fulfilling her dream of playing volleyball in high school. Once she made a choice, her vision, plan, balance, and action did the rest.

Jessica formed a mental picture of the player she wanted to become. Then she developed a plan to accomplish her vision. In her freshman year, when she had minimal playing time, she was an example to her teammates through her words and actions. She never let herself get discouraged. She became a leader because she "acted her way into a feeling." Once she had a vision and made a choice to act on it, she refused to give up.

Jessica was successful because she had: (1) a clear vision of what she wanted to accomplish; (2) a plan for accomplishing her goal; (3) a balanced work ethic that helped her make the most of practice time and summer vacations, and;

(4) a level of enthusiasm and desire that gave her the power to be successful on and off the court.

Jessica's "SAM" contained all the elements of a quality plan:

- It was **Specific**: Jessica wanted to be the setter and leader of her high school volleyball team. The summer she spent playing for Coach McGown was a specific strategy for acquiring the advanced skills and knowledge she needed to accomplish her goal.
- It was **Attainable**: John Wooden, the most successful coach in the history of college basketball, said, "Do not let what you cannot do interfere with what you can do." Jessica didn't give up when she realized she wasn't tall enough to play on the front row at the high school level. She chose a goal that allowed her to turn her disadvantage as a hitter into an advantage as a setter. Through hard work and sacrifice she became an excellent server as well.
- It was **Measurable**: Jessica's game time increased as she brought *The Four Stones* into alignment in her life. When coaches trusted Jessica to do things she hadn't been able to do before—serving overhand, for example—she had further evidence of the progress she was making.

If you find that you're creating excuses for not putting your plan into motion, the best way to overcome uncertainty and fear is simply to move forward. "Take the first step in faith," Martin Luther King Jr. said. "You don't have to see the whole staircase. Just take the first step."

SAM worked for Jessica. SAM worked for Sam. SAM will work for you if you put it to work in your life.

The Parable of the Four Stones

As leadership strategist Keith Craft explains, *alignment* comes before *assignment*. Jessica brought her *plan*, *balance*, and *action* into alignment with her *vision*. When *The Four Stones* came into alignment in Jessica's life, coaches started giving her the assignments she dreamed of.

CHAPTER 6

Balance

*I smiled to think God's greatness flowed around our
  incompleteness,—
Round our restlessness, His rest.*
  —*Elizabeth Barrett Browning*

To live satisfying lives, we must make our own choices. We must establish a *vision*; develop a quality *plan*; and take *action*. Many highly successful people, from Hollywood celebrities to professional athletes, have mastered these three stones.

The deadliest mistake "successful" people make is to ignore the Stone of Balance. From Texas billionaire Howard Hughes to the Australian actor Heath Ledger, faulty balance has been the ruin of many of the most gifted people that have lived and died in my lifetime.

Their backgrounds were different. They lived in different eras. But Hughes and Ledger followed the same path in life. Both men conquered Hollywood when they were young. Both climbed to the pinnacle of worldly success. But neither found lasting satisfaction.

Hughes was the richest man in the world, but his immense fortune couldn't buy him peace of mind. And although

Ledger appeared to be in better balance than those celebrities whose personal excesses fill the entertainment news, he was overwhelmed by loneliness and depression in the end.

Hughes died in Acapulco, Mexico. Ledger died in his Manhattan apartment. In reality, they died in the same place—off the path of God's best for their lives.

The Lifestyle of a Corporate Warrior

Both Howard Hughes and Heath Ledger were known as tireless workers. Hughes was an obsessive perfectionist when he arrived in Hollywood; by the time he left, he was just obsessed. Ledger was obsessed with stretching his limits as an actor.

Most of the business people I have known fall into the trap of believing they won't be successful if they aren't working long hours. For many years, I was in the same trap. When I was President and CEO of my former company my normal workday started at 8:00 AM and rarely ended before midnight. I worked at least half a day every Saturday, and sometimes on Sunday as well.

My body was usually in church on Sunday, but my mind was somewhere else. Even in church, I would constantly open my notebook to scribble down ideas for making my company grow.

My wife was CFO. We both led frantic lives. We ate most of our meals together when I wasn't on the road, but even at mealtime we talked about business. For over 15 years, the corporation consumed our life.

On January 14, 2004, I left Houston to deliver a speech in Belgium. I landed on the morning of January 15, delivered the speech, and caught a return flight to Montreal, Canada. By the time my flight landed in Montreal, my back was sore from sitting in a plane for two days. When I stood up, some-

The Parable of the Four Stones

thing happened. I felt a "click," and then another "click," as if dominos were tipping over somewhere inside my back.

The pain in my lower back was sharp, but I forced myself out of the plane and through the terminal to the baggage claim area, where my driver met me. The pain was getting worse: I could hardly breathe. My driver picked up my bags and loaded them—and me—into the car. He took me to my hotel and arranged to have my bags delivered to my room.

In my room, I slipped out of my clothes and into a tub of hot water. It felt great. It was -20° C outside; I was hurting and cold. I struggled to lift myself out of the tub. I managed to get my pajamas on before I got into bed. I stayed there for two days. The slightest movement caused pain to shoot through my lower back.

I was in Montreal to attend a conference and to deliver another speech. How was I going to give a speech in my condition? I could hardly get out of bed. The pain was unbearable. I had room service deliver soup and Tylenol, which sustained me during the long weekend.

On Monday I found a way to get dressed and attend the meeting. I could barely move my left leg. The pain hadn't let up at all. The Tylenol wasn't doing me any good now. The two days at the conference were like torture. I spent most of my time in my room, surviving on sheer grit.

On Tuesday night I flew across Canada to Edmonton, Alberta, for a three-day training session. Another flight was the last thing my back needed, but the session had been in the planning stages for months. Rescheduling would have cost me time and money. The people in Edmonton were as helpful as they could be when they realized how much pain I was in. Getting in and out of vehicles on the ground was making my condition worse, and I knew it. But I was a corporate warrior: I wasn't going to let "a little backache" stop me.

I flew back to Houston on Friday. My driver met me at the airport. I knew I would have a lot of explaining to do when I got home. As soon as Kim saw me, she knew I hadn't told her the truth about my "little backache." I hadn't told her how bad the pain really was. I stayed in bed all weekend.

My wife had broken an ankle roller-skating with our grandchildren while I was in Belgium. She was in pain herself, but that didn't stop her from taking care of me.

The next week I spent most of my out-of-bed time in doctors' offices. An MRI showed I had three injured discs in my lower back. That explained the "clicks" I heard when I stood up after my flight landed in Montreal. After a series of tests, doctors recommended surgery to repair the damaged discs.

Realigning My Priorities

I was ready to try anything to avoid back surgery. Lying in bed, watching a TV channel I never get—the signal was clear that day—I saw an advertisement for a new procedure to treat back problems without surgery. In the ad, a person with a problem similar to mine was renewed without surgery. I called the number on the screen the next morning.

I made an appointment and found out about the procedure. It would be a long drive: The only place in Houston that offered the service was 60 miles from my home. I would have to make a one-hour drive in heavy traffic two times a day.

I could only sit for 15 to 20 minutes at a time; then I had to walk for at least 15 minutes. What normally would have been a one-hour drive became a two-hour drive in my condition—a four-hour round trip.

I made the trip every day for six weeks. Then I started physical therapy. By the time the treatment phase was over, my back was as good as new. On November 6, 2004, my doctor told me I could resume my normal activity.

The Parable of the Four Stones

My health problems weren't behind me yet. Ten days later, I had an allergic reaction that caused a bad sneezing attack while I was sitting in my office.

It started as a burning sensation in my right arm. Over the next couple of days I felt more and more pain in my arm. The more pain I felt, the less I could move my arm. The pain got so bad that I couldn't grasp anything with my fingers. I visited a chiropractor. He did his best to work the pain out, but nothing helped.

After that I visited my personal doctor, who sent me to a specialist. On December 16, 2004, I was told I would probably lose the use of my arm permanently. I had emergency surgery the next day.

During my sneezing attack, I had splintered a bone in my neck. A bone chip hit a nerve in my arm, which was responsible for the pain and loss of control in my fingers. The specialist removed the bone chip and rebuilt my disc with a piece of bone taken from my right thigh. When I woke up, I could move my arm again. My neck was fine, but I had the worst pain in my leg—and no voice.

The pain in my leg went away over the next few days, but my voice got worse and worse. A week after my emergency surgery, I still hadn't recovered my voice. I could barely whisper.

I couldn't travel or leave the house. My world was reduced to wherever I could connect my two computers at home. I couldn't speak for four months. In June 2005, six months after surgery, I was given permission to travel again.

I had been forced to undergo a total lifestyle change. I reduced my workload by at least 60% for over a year. While I was recovering at home, I ran my company from my computer.

Working at home gave me the opportunity to spend more time with my wife, my family, and my friends. Not only did my relationship with my wife improve, but I discovered that I could still accomplish a lot of work.

During my rehabilitation, I had time to reflect on the values that had given my life meaning in the past. I had plenty of time to question the premise that business people have to be workaholics to succeed.

I learned that people can be successful in business without destroying their health and relationships. As Brian Tracy explains, "Just as your car runs more smoothly and requires less energy to go faster and farther when the wheels are in perfect alignment, you perform better when your thoughts, feelings, emotions, goals, and values are in balance."

We choose the way we live: Lifestyle is a choice, not a requirement. Most business people never make a choice to bring their lives into balance. They fall into the trap of believing that career advancement is what gives value and meaning to life.

The reality is just the opposite: When business people maintain balance in their lives, they create more value for their companies and build more satisfying relationships with the people they love.

I had to lose my balance to learn how important balance is.

How's Your Balance?

After moving to the Dallas area and getting involved in my new church, I met a man that has become my personal wellness coach and one of the best friends I have had in life, Dr. Joe Fawcett.

Dr. Joe and I have lunch together a few times each month. He's a walking encyclopedia of health and wellness. Whenever I need to tap into his wisdom and experience, I visit his website at www.powertobewell.com.

The Parable of the Four Stones

At one of our lunches, I expressed my belief that balance is the key to staying on God's path for our lives. My comment caused a light bulb to turn on over his head. His response is an in-depth look at the Stone of Balance from the perspective of a health and wellness expert:

"Jeff, when someone is sick, has a long-term illness, or some kind of health issue that's robbing their life of energy," Dr. Joe began, "we doctors say that the body is *out of balance*... it's out of 'ease'... it's *imbalanced* like a flat tire on a vehicle that doesn't go anywhere. Another way of seeing it is in the word 'dis-ease'... disease. The prefix 'dis' means 'negative' and 'ease' means 'absence of difficulty.' So disease occurs when someone's health is *out of balance*, causing them to experience various negative degrees of 'difficulty' in their body or mind. And it's always due to something in the person's life being *out of balance* because of a *choice* they made. Keep in mind that the marvelous internal biochemical system of our body is always seeking 'homeostasis.' That's a fancy medical word for *'balance.'*

"In fact, everything in nature and in the universe seeks to maintain *balance*. You, for example: If you don't exercise at least 30 minutes a day, three days a week, then all kinds of bad things will begin to happen to you over time. And eventually, because you didn't have a *balanced*, routine lifestyle of consistent exercising, you'll suffer a 'disease' of some kind, somewhere in your body, sometime in your life—usually in your 40s or 50s, when you're entering the prime of life and you should be feeling and looking good. You don't want to go through the best part of your life *'out of balance.'* A lack of balance isn't just expensive and painful—it's life-shortening.

"Consider this: Prolonged bad stress is a killer. This kind of stress, which you allow and actually invite into your body or mind, dramatically throws you *out of balance*. 80% of all illnesses can be traced back to some kind of prolonged bad stress. By the way, safe and sane exercising is a tremendous stress buster.

"As a Doctor of Chiropractic and a wellness coach, I see it all the time: men and women so *out of balance* that negative stress is literally killing them, either slowly or quickly. And it can all be stopped: Most of the time the *imbalance* can be brought back into *balance*.

"Jeff, balanced exercise, balanced nutrition, and balanced sleep make up the Physical Spoke on my Wellness Wheel. If one of these three things is out of *balance*, it's not too long before it affects the other two. But not only will it affect the Physical Spoke—it will also have a bad effect on the other eight Spokes that make up my Wheel of Wellness.

"Who's in the hub of the wheel? That's up to you. I always picture my Wellness Wheel with a question mark inside the hub. Only one thing can be there: *you* or *your relationship with God*. You choose what to put in the center of your life. My experience has taught me that if you put yourself in the hub, you're headed for huge troubles.

"Again, wellness is all about *balance*. If any of the three components of a Spoke breaks, the whole Wellness Wheel gets *out of balance*. It won't be long until that person wobbles into the deep ditch I call 'dis-ease,' simply because they made *choices*—knowingly or unknowingly—to be *out of balance* with life the way it's supposed to be lived. So, you see, *balance* is the critical aspect of life: When we lose our balance, everything else falls with it.

"Like I always say, it's your *choice*: You do have the power to be well. But it takes accountability. That's why everyone who wants *balance* in their life needs a team that works together to achieve and maintain *balance*. And a vital part of that team is the Wellness Coach—a specialist who teaches you to set and reach new goals for your personal health and wellness. Like any good coach, a wellness coach encourages you to do more than you could have done on your own."

From an experienced doctor's viewpoint, balance is critical to good health. Balance gives us peace of mind. Balance gives us the assurance and confidence to try new options and make new choices. We don't have to be sick as we grow older if we maintain balance in our body throughout life.

The Nine Spokes of Dr. Joe's Wellness Wheel:

Physical: Exercise, Nutrition, Sleep
Psychological: Stress, Change, Adaptation
Eternal: Preparation, Dying, Death
Social: Values, Priorities, Morals
Environmental: Resources, Pollution, Stewardship
Spiritual: Prayer, Faith, Worship
Mental: Intellect, Will, Emotions
Vocational: Finances, Work, Leisure
Relational: Family, Church, Community

Balance is the stone that most people leave out of their lives. We can have a Vision. We can work to establish a Plan. We can jump right onto the Stone of Action. But if we haven't achieved Balance in our life, we fall off the stone, get swept away by our obstacle, and find ourselves back on the path of default.

In Part 3 of *The Four Stones*, Sam and Mrs. Livingstone are working in the garden. Mrs. Livingstone has been trying to remember something that John Angler said the night before he left Copyville.

"I know what he said," Sam tells his mother.

"What was it?" she asks.

"He said, 'God made us to be empty without him.' He said we'll never be satisfied until we discover God's path for our lives."

In the language of Dr. Joe Fawcett's Wellness model, God made our "wheels" to be unbalanced without him. When we make our relationship with God our number one priority in life, we become free people and powerful people.

Free to consider new options, free to make new choices, free to be well, and free to change the path we're on.

CHAPTER 7

Action

"Leadership is a potent combination of strategy and character. But if you must be without one, be without the strategy."
—Norman Schwarzkopf

In Part 4 of *The Four Stones*, Sam is ready to cross the stream. He steps across the first three stones with confidence. Then, with one foot on the third stone and the other foot on the last stone, he hesitates.

The longer he stays stuck on the last stone, the more dangerous his situation becomes. *This is the worst position I could be in,* Sam says to himself. His legs are starting to ache. *I'll never reach the bank if my legs cramp up. How did I get myself in this position?* For a moment, Sam thinks he isn't going to make it.

Sam falls into the trap of focusing on his feelings when he should be focusing on his next action. As long as his inner voice is in control of the dialogue, Sam is in trouble. Then he remembers what John Angler taught him.

"I still have to take the last step," he says out loud.

The stream is just an obstacle in Sam's path; it isn't the real enemy. Sam's real enemy is the stream of negative thoughts rushing through his head. Sam stops thinking about the surging water. He stops thinking about the pain in his legs. He lifts his left foot off the Stone of Balance. Pushing off the Stone of Action with his right foot, his momentum carries him safely onto the bank of the stream.

Ready...Fire...Aim!

Ralph Waldo Emerson said, "As long as a man stands in his own way, everything seems to be in his way." When Sam stopped listening to his inner voice, he was able to get out of his own way and take the last step.

By crossing the stream, Sam wins the biggest battle in life—the battle against himself. By learning how to control his inner thought process, Sam learns how to control the results he gets in life.

It's important to understand the difference between our *intuition* and our *inner voice*. The American Heritage College Dictionary defines intuition as "the act or faculty of knowing or sensing without the use of rational processes." Psychologists call this "thin slicing," the ability to make accurate split-second decisions based on a small amount of information.

"Thin slicing" is what tells an NFL quarterback whether to wait for a receiver to pull away from a defender or to put the ball under his arm and run. It tells a police officer whether to fire at a young man who pulls his hand out of a coat pocket in a dark alley.

As every football coach and police commissioner knows, intuition is far from infallible. The best quarterbacks sometimes throw an interception when they should have held onto the ball. Experienced police officers sometimes shoot an innocent suspect when they should have waited a split-second longer before deciding whether to pull the trigger.

The Parable of the Four Stones

Intuition is far more important in business than most people realize. Research in the psychology of decision making suggests that successful business executives base important choices more on intuition than on rational analysis of business data.

When companies grow and stock values increase, you can be sure that the man or woman at the top is making choices based on intuition, passion, and pride. But as every stockholder knows, business leaders are only human: Faulty intuition often leads to bad decisions and business mistakes that cost millions of dollars. As the Bible tells us, pride comes before the fall.

As a business executive, I prided myself on my quick judgments, fast decisions, and intuition. My decision-making process as the CEO of a major corporation was "Ready-Fire-Aim." The inherent danger in this process is that it carries with it increased risk of making fatal judgment errors and alienating the people around you.

Intuition is a powerful tool, but it's a two-edged sword. The real danger of a "Ready-Fire-Aim" approach is that short-term success almost always conceals serious shortcomings in the planning process. My vision for the company can be sound, but poor planning will lead to bad results in the long run. A "Ready-Fire-Aim" approach always makes things happen, but the outcomes aren't always the ones I wanted.

I have learned to balance my thought processes and decision making: I plan before I take action. The time for careful planning and analysis is when we're standing on the Stones of Plan and Balance. As soon as we step onto the Stone of Action, it's time to stop analyzing. If we don't control our inner dialogue and concentrate on moving forward, we fall into the "paralysis-by-analysis" trap, just like Sam did when he hesitated on the last stone.

Your inner dialogue—the one you carry on with yourself inside your own head—is almost always negative. Our

The Parable of the Four Stones

minds are storage bins for everything we see and hear. If your parents constantly reminded you when you were growing up that standing in a draft of cold air or getting drenched in a rainstorm causes colds, you probably suffer cold symptoms every time you get wet.

Scientists learned a long time ago that colds are caused by viruses. Getting wet or standing in a cold draft doesn't give you a cold; only viruses cause colds. When our immune systems are working correctly, we aren't even affected by the presence of ordinary viruses and bacteria. When all systems are working as they should, common viruses and bacteria don't make us sick.

When healthy people catch a cold or get the flu, it's because something else triggered the onset of symptoms. Research shows that stress is the biggest detonator of disease known to science. The "bad stress" that Dr. Joe Fawcett talked about in the last chapter is the most common detonator of illness. Studies of distance runners, for example, show that marathoners are more likely to come down with a cold or flu after completing a race. The stress of competition is often enough to detonate illnesses in professional distance runners, who are among the healthiest people alive.

When people say things like, "I think I'm coming down with something," they're usually coughing and sneezing the next time you see them. That doesn't mean they don't have a virus in their body. But it usually means that the onset of symptoms was triggered by their internal thought processes.

People literally make themselves sick and worry themselves to death.

It's impossible to avoid negative thoughts entirely: Our minds are simply too efficient at storing data. You might not like the advertising jingle or pop song you heard in the shopping mall, but you hear the lyrics over and over again in your head all day long.

Martin Luther was right when he said you can't stop birds from flying over your head, but you can prevent them from building a nest in it. How do you keep negativity from building a nest in your mind? The only way to control negative thoughts is by feeding your brain the right food.

The English cardiologist Martyn Lloyd-Jones said, "Most unhappiness in life is due to the fact that you are listening to yourself rather than talking to yourself."

Martyn Lloyd-Jones is also a clergyman: He knows that the best way to turn off our negative inner dialogue is to study the Bible. When you catch yourself paying attention to the voice that says you're going to get sick, you're going to fail, or you're not going to be good enough, the best way to take control of your thoughts is to "talk to yourself" in God's language.

Like explorers on a jungle trail, we must be careful of what lies hidden in the underbrush. Human intuition is a powerful tool, but it's a double-edged sword. And our inner voice is like a dangerous predator, always waiting to pounce on us from behind.

The Bible is the only guide that never fails to take us in the right direction. Believing what the Bible says is the first step toward seeing ourselves as God sees us. And when we see each other as God sees us, "we have the mind of Christ."

When that happens, nothing on earth can steal our peace of mind and joy from us.

Overcoming Yourself

One of the biggest obstacles people face when they need to make a choice is their internal thought process. I have known extremely capable and talented people who could overcome any obstacle when it came to helping someone else, but they couldn't make the right decisions about important things in their own lives.

The biggest source of misinformation in the world is our own inner voice. If we believe all the negative things our inner voice tells us about ourselves, we condemn ourselves to face life without confidence and without courage.

Watching my son Martin win the battle against himself was an experience I'll cherish for the rest of my life. Martin was a sports fanatic who fell in love with tennis in junior high school. He watched tennis, studied tennis, and lived tennis. We hired good coaches to teach him, to challenge him, and to improve his skills.

Martin worked harder than most other teenagers to improve his game. He spent several weeks in training at Nick Bollettieri's IMG Academy in Bradenton, Florida, the number one tennis institute in the world. Andre Agassi, Pete Sampras, Boris Becker, Bjorn Borg, and the Williams sisters (Venus and Serena) are all alumni of Nick Bollettieri's IMG Academy.

Martin would spend hours and hours on the tennis court, and he had the tan to prove it. He carried a dozen rackets in his bag. He could wear out a pair of expensive tennis shoes in a week. Tennis was his life.

Martin's coaches were impressed with his technique, his commitment, and his intensity. Few players could match up with Martin in a practice session. Martin was unbeatable in practice, but something happened when he played a match. He wasn't the same person when the points counted.

Something happened to Martin when a real game began: He didn't think he could win. Before a match, Martin would do his best to prepare himself mentally. But his fear of losing prevented him from reaching his full potential as a player.

When Martin was 15 years old, the Brewer family drove across Houston on a typical tennis weekend. I wondered if Martin would be ready to attack his opponent from the opening serve. Would he take control of the game by playing as aggressively and confidently as he always played in prac-

The Parable of the Four Stones

tice, or would he let his opponent dictate the tempo and style of play?

Martin's first opponent that weekend was a less experienced player. It should have been an easy match-up for Martin. But everything that coaches and analysts say is true: Tennis is a mental game as much as it's a physical game.

Martin didn't bring his best game that day; the match quickly got out of hand. Though Martin was giving it his best effort, he lost the first set 0-6. Martin's opponent won the first five games of the second set. When Martin lost the first three points of Game 6, it was match point.

Kim and I tried everything we could think of to encourage our son, but nothing worked.

"You can do it!" Kim shouted after every point. "Slow down. Take your time."

"I'm trying," Martin answered from time to time.

"Come on!" he said to himself, beating the face of his racket with the palm of his hand, spurring himself into action like a rider spurs a horse.

We were frustrated parents who knew our son's potential. We didn't understand why he couldn't perform as well in a match as he always did in practice.

"Idiot," Martin blurted out loud enough for everyone to hear after slamming a ball into the net. He bounced his racket off the top of his head as he prepared for the next point.

Martin was beginning to hit balls out of bounds on purpose, just to let off steam.

"Stupid," he said, loud enough for everyone to hear.

Martin's coach kept looking for the right button to push. He reminded Martin of his accomplishments on the practice court, his strengths, how to move his feet, how to think. He tried to keep Martin focused on the little things: where to place his serve, when to charge the net, when to make a passing shot.

Martin was obviously frustrated. He hadn't won a single game. It was match point now: Martin was only one point away from losing the match. The situation looked hopeless.

"Think," Kim said, speaking more softly now, as if Martin didn't need to hear the words to know what his mother was saying.

"Focus," I added, practically whispering to myself.

Martin saved match point. Then he won the next point... and the next... and the next. He fought all the way back to win the game, the set, and the next set.

Martin had clawed his way back to win the match! In all, he won three matches on Saturday and two matches on Sunday to win the tournament.

What caused the tide to turn? The key was the transformation in Martin's self-image. During his remarkable comeback, Martin made a choice to see himself as a winner.

When he lost a point, he said, "Good shot." Then he forgot about the point he had just lost and focused on the next point. For the first time in his life, Martin was "in the zone," a state of peak performance that champion athletes attain when they stop thinking about winning or losing and submerge themselves in the moment.

When athletes are in the zone, they no longer think about the score. They aren't aware of the crowd. Their focus is so intense that they're able to block out everything except the point they're playing.

Professional athletes describe "being in the zone" as a state of total concentration in which their bodies reach a level of peak performance even as their minds become more relaxed. When an athlete is in the zone, body and mind are perfectly synchronized.

Athletes in this state of total concentration and perfect balance seem to glide effortlessly through the game. They perform at their physical peak and, at the same time, experience peak enjoyment of their sport.

Martin entered "the zone" when he saved match point, and he stayed there the rest of the weekend. The more games Martin won, the more he smiled. He was exhausted, but his energy level reached new heights as he kept on winning. His body posture improved and his confidence increased with every stroke of the racket. He encouraged the losers after each match, telling them how good they were.

Standing tall, he carried his racket bag over his shoulder instead of letting it droop by his side. He saw himself differently at the end of the tournament, and we all saw a different Martin. There was a glow about him. He was willing to discuss the technical aspects of his game; he never wanted to talk about them before.

Martin played tennis all four years that he attended Pearland High School. He won a lot of matches and lost some too. In victory and in defeat, he was a leader to himself and to others. He was a disciplined, dedicated player who sought out opportunities to encourage teammates and opponents alike.

Martin went on to play tennis for San Jacinto College. After his graduation, he put down the competitive rackets to follow a different path. He is a successful businessman today because of the choices he makes. He still follows a path of purpose because he made a decision one day to change his mental picture of himself.

Answering the Big Questions

John told Sam he would be ready to cross the stream when he learned how to lead himself. I constantly remind myself to "act my way into a feeling instead of feeling my way into an action." I don't always feel like taking the next step. But if I have a vision and a balanced plan, I can take action even though I don't feel like it.

You're implementing *The Four Stones* in your life when you have clear answers to the Big Questions:

1. **Vision:** Where are you going? What outcome do you want? What would make you—and the people you want to serve—happy?
2. **Plan:** How will you get there?
3. **Balance:** Who do you need to become to achieve your vision?
4. **Action:** Are you learning how to lead yourself?

Your answer to Question #3 gives you the Big Picture for your life: Who am I? Why do I have the vision I have? Am I doing what I need to do to be transformed into the kind of person that can accomplish this vision?

When your answers to these questions are clear, every action you take will move you closer to your goal. You'll no longer waste time and energy rehashing yesterday's choices and worrying about what will happen tomorrow. You'll be sure of where you want to go, how you plan to get there, and the person you must become to achieve your dream.

God's vision for your life is not a problem-free life, but a victorious life. Satisfaction and peace of mind are determined by two things: your attitude and your choice of who to put in the center of your life.

That's really all there is to it. If God isn't in your success, no amount of success will satisfy you.

CHAPTER 8

Cocoon Season

"The highest reward for a person's toil is not what he gets for it, but what he becomes by it."
—John Ruskin

In Part 2 of *The Four Stones*, John Angler uses a cocoon to explain how God transforms people.

"God wants to give us new minds here on earth," he tells Sam. "Butterflies are God's way of saying, 'This is just a small preview of what I'm turning you into.'"

Sam gets the point: To accomplish his vision, he must become a new person:

I can't sit around and wait for the change to happen first and then cross the stream. I have to cross the stream and get on my right path first, then God will have something to work with (my new mind) so he can change the way I think and then I'll be able to lead the blind because I won't be blind anymore.

Sam crosses the stream and follows his path of purpose. A shepherd has been waiting for him to come.

"People are more than what they appear to be," the shepherd tells Sam. "Didn't John Angler teach you that?"

Sam isn't stumped by riddles anymore. Like Martin and Jessica, he has learned how to lead himself, and he is enjoying the journey.

Ruskin was right: Sam, Martin, and Jessica all received the "highest reward"—not what they got for their toil, but what they became by it.

Transactional vs. Transformational Living

In a consumer society, the activity that defines most people's lives is the "deal"—the act of buying and selling goods and services. No matter how different you and I are, shopping is the one thing we have in common: We can't satisfy basic needs like food, clothing, and shelter without planning and completing simple economic transactions every day.

We go to a store because we want something the store sells. We track it down in the aisles; pick it off the shelf; take it to the front of the store; wait for our turn in the checkout line (not nearly as much fun as tracking it down was); and exchange our hard-earned dollars for the product. End of transaction.

Life by default is like being in a never-ending transaction mode. We move from one situation to another not as a result of our conscious choices, but by default. Having failed to make our own decisions, we come to the place where we are today because we didn't have a vision for our lives. Without a vision and without a plan, we have no way to take actions to change our course in life.

We are what we are and have what we have because of our choices, whether we're conscious of the choices we make or not. Day after day, we make transactions to move from one situation to another. It's not the best way to live, but for 97% of the world's population, this is as good as it gets.

Being "transformational" means that I live for a cause larger than myself. I make decisions based on the long-term good of the people I serve: My vision is something that creates benefits for others, not just for me. My plans and my actions are aligned with my vision. This is living life by design.

Transformation is a difficult concept to understand in a society like ours, one that values free will above all other things. But our highest calling in life is serving others: If we are to become all that we ought to be, we must live our life for a transformational cause.

My pastor at CCC, Keith Craft, helped me discover my full potential by teaching me how God transforms people through the power of the Bible. One of the most astonishing ideas in history is the Biblical "recipe" for elevating our life by elevating the way we think:

> "And so, dear brothers and sisters, I plead with you to give your bodies to God because of all he has done for you. Let them be a living and holy sacrifice—the kind he will find acceptable. This is truly the way to worship him. Don't copy the behavior and customs of this world, but let God transform you into a new person by changing the way you think. Then you will learn to know God's will for you, which is good and pleasing and perfect" (Romans 12:1-2).

Life by design is a real possibility. Based on this passage in Romans alone, God guarantees that you will discover his vision for your life if you just believe what the Bible says. And if you act on that vision, God guarantees that his "good and pleasing and perfect" plan will fill your life with lasting satisfaction.

The Parable of the Four Stones

Like Sam, Martin, and Jessica, I have been going through a period of transformation in my life. God is transforming me from a high-strung corporate mover and shaker into a person he can use for his purpose. I'm learning how to stay on God's path instead of my own self-directed path.

When Kim and I were senior executives at the analytical instrumentation company we moved our top sales person, Jeremy Skidmore, from Houston to Dallas. Jeremy is also our son-in-law. When my wife and I visited our daughter and son-in-law in the Dallas area, we attended Celebration Covenant Church in McKinney. Every time Kim and I attended a service at CCC, we left with a deeper understanding of our relationship with God. We talked about the services, bought the CD series and listened to the messages.

I kept Pastor Keith Craft's CDs in my bus, a 40-foot, over-the-road tour bus that my company used for demonstrating our analytical instruments to laboratories across the U.S. A chauffeur drove the bus when I wasn't available. I often drove it myself and participated in the demonstrations with my sales people. I loved traveling coast to coast. I loved driving the bus and I loved being in front of my customers. As I drove from one side of the United States to the other, I listened to Keith's messages over and over again.

As we listened and learned, Kim and I began to realize something. Even though we had reached the pinnacle of business success, we knew there was more. We hadn't reached the "Peak of Satisfaction" that John Angler shows Sam in Part 4 of *The Four Stones*.

When we visited our daughter and son-in-law, we saw a profound change in their attitudes and priorities. We even noticed a change in Lindy, our oldest granddaughter. Jeremy's work ethic was transformed from good to great; the sharp edges that once defined his personality disappeared; his sales and self-confidence soared.

Jeremy's attitude changed: He began leading himself. He was more positive in his outlook and encouraged others to be positive. He became more involved in church and family. As Kim and I watched Jeremy reach new heights, we asked God for a church like CCC in Houston. We didn't know it then, but God was already preparing the way for our relocation to McKinney.

God answers prayers: He answered ours. He literally interrupted our lives to push us out of our comfort zones. If he hadn't, we wouldn't have had the opportunity to experience the fullness of joy that comes from a closer relationship with him.

Cure vs. Process

Seth Godin is the founder and CEO of www.squidoo.com. A bestselling author and marketing consultant, he understands consumer behavior as well as anyone in the world today.

As he pointed out in a recent blog post, consumers don't want a "process" or a "best effort." They want a cure. When people buy something, he explains, all they really care about is whether it will solve their problems:

> "Doctors, of course, can rarely provide a cure. Neither can accountants or marketing consultants. But that's what gets sold, cause that's what people want to buy. We fool ourselves constantly. We know, deep down (or not even so deep) that there's no real cure out there, but that's what we pay for anyway" (sethgodin.typepad.com, June 5, 2008).

Transactional living focuses on quick fixes. Seth is right about the first part: Consumers fool themselves constantly. As consumers, we fool ourselves every time we buy a "cure" in the hope that it will save us the time and trouble of going through a "process."

Seth is wrong about the second part. There is a "cure," but it isn't the type of cure that most consumers (and marketing consultants) think of as a cure, because it's really a process: the process that Paul described in Romans 12: 1-2.

Seth Godin's blog post would have been as relevant in 33 A.D. as it is today. If his message could be translated into ancient Greek and transported 2,000 years back in time, the apostle Paul would have understood exactly what Seth was talking about.

In temples and dusty markets all over the Roman Empire, people went shopping for salvation. They entered into a simple transaction to exchange their hard-earned denarios for omens, relics, and sacrifices to the temple gods. People were as adept at fooling themselves then as they are today. Roman gods and temple prostitutes didn't provide a cure, of course, but that's what people paid for anyway.

People in 33 A.D. had the same choice between "transactional" and "transformational" living that we have today. Just like today, people in 33 A.D. had two different "Christs" to choose from.

On one hand, there was a "Transformational" Christ (the one that Matthew, Mark, Luke, and John wrote about in the New Testament); on the other hand, there was a "Transactional" Christ (the one that a first-century religious sect known as "Gnostics" were telling people about).

The Gnostic gospels were discovered in Egypt in 1945. These ancient writings teach a method of salvation that is "transactional" in the same way that shopping for groceries is a transaction. Paul and other leaders of the early church were very much aware of the Gnostics and their teachings. The New Testament contains several warnings about false teachers and ministers, which clearly point to the first-century Gnostics.

The Gnostics taught that salvation is by "gnosis"—the ancient Greek word for "knowledge." How did Gnostics achieve "gnosis"? The Gnostic gospels don't explain how to become a Gnostic: Candidates had to discover this secret on their own.

The Christ of the Gnostic gospels points the way to "salvation," but it is the individual who "saves himself" by tapping into his own divine nature. Believers were given no clear instructions on how to do this. Being a Gnostic wasn't easy: Gnostics had no way to know if they were "saved" or not.

In the *Gospel of Mary of Magdala*, one of the Gnostic gospels, Jesus says, "There is no such thing as sin." Since there is no sin, the Gnostic Jesus is not a "savior," although his apostles call him that. He is a teacher, but one who is totally unlike the Jesus of the New Testament.

Another Gnostic document, *The Acts of John*, portrays Jesus as a non-human spiritual being who had the ability to project himself as if he were a hologram. According to this document, Jesus never left footprints and never blinked his eyes.

Save myself? Anyone who believes he can "save himself," as first-century Gnostics believed, might as well organize a 21st-century expedition to continue Ponce de Leon's quest for the Fountain of Youth.

The spirit of the Gnostic gospels is a spirit of pride: the spirit that led to the fall of Adam and Eve, the spirit that wants to be God—to have no authority or power above itself.

In the Gnostic gospels the "new life" is what we would call heightened "self-awareness" today. In the *Gospel of Thomas*, Jesus says, "Whoever finds the interpretations of these sayings will not experience death." (Elaine Pagels, *The Gnostic Gospels*, Vintage Books, 1979)

The problem with Gnosticism and New Age spirituality—which is simply first-century Gnosticism in 21st-century clothing—is that, without God's transforming power, there is no way for a person to achieve what these doctrines offer. The message of the Cross teaches us that we cannot save ourselves. We need a Savior.

The Gnostic says, "I don't need a savior. I am self-sufficient. I can solve my own problems. Just show me where to buy the cure."

The Gnostic Jesus doesn't transform his followers. He simply gives them a sales plan. In the Gnostic gospels, Jesus is portrayed as a first-century Feng Shui coach who teaches people how to buy spiritual satisfaction. The seed of New Age religion is in the Gnostic message: "Discover the god within you."

The Gnostic "Christ" is a Jesus we don't know and can't trust. How different this is from New Testament Christianity, in which men and women are saved by faith in Christ as their Redeemer.

Christ's teachings brought about lasting change. When the Christ of the New Testament spoke, a person's whole attitude was transformed on the spot. The change comes when God's spirit breaks through the "frozen sea within us." When Christ lives in a human heart, people change in ways that take them totally by surprise.

There are two miracles in the Bible you can stake your life on: the resurrection of Christ and the transformation of people like Paul and the apostles. The power that God used to bring Christ back from the dead is the same power that will make you a new person if you let God change the way you think.

Take the Last Step

The choice between the two Christs has made people stumble for the last 2,000 years. The life of Charles Dickens, the greatest novelist in the English language, is a case study of a man who stumbled on the Stone of Christ. The creator of Oliver Twist and the Artful Dodger might well be the most famous admirer of Christ who never made the right decision about the man he so admired.

Dickens is the author of one of the most beautiful transformation stories in world literature: *A Christmas Carol*, the tale of Ebenezer Scrooge. Who hasn't been moved to tears by one of the many film versions of the story? Scrooge wakes up on Christmas morning with a purpose to live for. He is ready to spread happiness throughout the land and ready to be happy himself. But has Scrooge really been transformed?

Not at all. He simply made a deal with a ghost. It's the noblest deal any man or woman can ever make, but it's a transaction just the same. Scrooge makes a promise to the last Spirit of Christmas: He will make amends for his wasted life by doing as much good as he can for others. Scrooge keeps his promise; he becomes the most generous man in all England. But he has not been transformed from within.

Dickens hoped to make the same deal with God that Scrooge makes with the ghost. Twenty-one years before his death, he wrote *The Life of Our Lord*, a retelling of the life of Christ in language that his children could understand. His Christ is a transactional Christ: Dickens encouraged his children to be like Christ, but there is no certainty of salvation in the pages of his book. Throughout the manuscript, Dickens implies that people go to heaven because of their good deeds rather than their faith in Christ.

The "Good News" of the New Testament is that salvation is available to all who choose to receive it. As far as we know, Dickens was never sure of his salvation. His last will and testament included a section in which he asked Jesus Christ to have mercy on his soul. (Charles Dickens, *The Life of Our Lord*, foreword and appendix by Dr. D. James Kennedy: Westminster Press, 1986)

Though we have no way to know for sure (Dickens could have made a decision for Christ on his death bed), his last will suggests that he never prayed to God for forgiveness, nor is it likely that he ever received Christ as his Redeemer.

Dickens admired Christ and taught his children to be like Christ. But as far as we know, he never took the last step.

The full meaning of Sam's words at the stream should be clear now.

"The last stone is action," he said, grasping the lesson that John Angler wanted him to learn. "Vision, planning, and balance can take you close enough to the other side that you can almost touch it. But you still have to take the last step."

Vision, planning, and balance can take people close enough to their dream that they can "almost touch it." They might believe, as Dickens seemed to believe, that God occupies an important place in their lives. But they still have to make a decision about the two Christs: They must decide whether Christ was just a good man and a wise teacher, or the living God that stepped down from heaven into human history.

Like Sam said, "You still have to take the last step."

And when you take it, you discover the "cure" the whole world is looking for: the process that turns you into a new person by changing the way you think.

CHAPTER 9

On This Rock

"You have made us for yourself, O Lord, and our heart is restless until it rests in you."
—Augustine, *Confessions*

What would life be like if satisfaction was guaranteed? I asked this question at the beginning of our journey. I hope this book has helped you to find the answer.

Satisfaction is a state of mind that exists when you discover God's "good and pleasing and perfect" plan for your life. When your relationship with God replaces "you" in the hub of your life, peace of mind replaces doubt, uncertainty, and fear.

Mihaly Csikszentmihalyi is the author of *Flow: The Psychology of Optimal Experience*. (HarperCollins Publishers, 1990) Csikszentmihalyi has devoted his life to the scientific study of peak performance—the state that athletes call "being in the zone." *Flow* offers readers "steps toward enhancing the quality of life."

After decades of research in the psychology of happiness, Csikszentmihalyi made a simple discovery: "People who learn to control inner experience will be able to determine the quality of their lives, which is as close as any of us can come to being happy."

He is right about the first part. The quality of our lives depends on learning to control our inner experience, which is just another way to say that happiness depends on learning how to "act your way into a feeling instead of feeling your way into an action," as John Angler taught Sam. Satisfaction in life depends on learning how to lead ourselves, which is how we "learn to control inner experience."

But Csikszentmihalyi is wrong about the second part: We can come closer than that. The "Flow Experience" can take people close enough to the shore of their dreams that they can almost touch it, but it can't take people all the way across. It can provide them with a certain kind of happiness for a season, but it can never provide lasting satisfaction.

Only one thing can do that.

I was like so many other young people in the 1960s and 70s. I got "saved" at least a dozen times a year. I got saved all over again every time we had a "Vacation Bible School," and even when I was invited to Vacation Bible School at my friends' churches. These events were full of emotion and good intentions, but none of them changed my life.

I grew up in an Assemblies of God church that my parents attended. We drove from Pasadena to Baytown, Texas, every Sunday morning for Sunday school and church. When I was in first or second grade, I was kicked out of Sunday school for singing the Busch Bavarian beer song, a popular TV commercial with a catchy tune.

My parents stopped attending church. I never knew why. As their attendance tailed off, I stopped going to church too. I attended services with friends sometimes, but not very often. In high school I became well-known locally as a musician with my own band. I played guitar; I knew a lot of quality musicians; and I had professional sound equipment.

The Parable of the Four Stones

In the early 1970s church youth choirs were performing lots of musicals. The best youth groups were also going on tour. I attended whatever church offered me the most money for the use of my equipment and for providing live musicians for the musical they were presenting. I was well connected with tour-bus drivers, so I frequently arranged the transportation for tours. I attended church services but I didn't allow myself to be restricted by the rules of the youth group. They wanted me; I wanted the money. I was going to live by my own rules.

When I was 18 years old, I went to Nashville, Tennessee, on a Nazarene Youth Choir tour. I had arranged the bus for the group and I knew the driver well. We spent Saturday evening together at a local bar. I wasn't a bad guy; I just liked to have a drink or two, especially if it made me look "important" or "unique." I liked having that "rebellious" look, even though I wasn't much of a rebel.

The next day we presented the musical in church. It was different this time. It wasn't "just another musical." The songs spoke to my spirit as they never had before. At the end of the service, I put down my guitar and went to the altar. If I had just won an Oscar, people couldn't have been happier for me. Members of the youth group and the group's adult sponsors gathered around me to pray. This time it was real.

I gave my life to Christ that day and I have never looked back. I continued to play in youth musicals, but I didn't hire myself and my equipment out anymore. I stayed with the Nazarene Youth Group from Pasadena, Texas, for several years after my salvation in Nashville.

I married the most beautiful alto singer in the group. My wife and I became the youth leaders at the church. We led our own youth musicals and introduced innovations in our music ministry that were adopted by other churches in our area.

After that Sunday in Nashville, Tennessee, the biggest transformation in me was my desire to live right in the eyes of God. I stopped hanging out at the bars; I stopped trying to look like a rebel. I discovered that getting involved in church didn't mean I had to lose my uniqueness. Going to church became a privilege for me, instead of something I had to do.

Living a disciplined life used to be a struggle for me. I always equated "discipline" with the things I didn't want to do. Discipline meant gritting your teeth, bearing down as hard as you could, and forcing yourself to do the hardest and least enjoyable parts of a job. Then one day I stopped thinking in terms of "discipline" and started thinking in terms of "responsibility." I realized I could be "responsible" to lead myself based on my new thought processes.

Now that I'm living life by design, I have the *privilege* to be responsible for my choices. I *choose* to have a vision for my life; I *choose* to make plans to accomplish my vision; I *choose* to take specific actions to move closer to my goals.

The path of default is a way of life that encourages people to blame others for their broken dreams and empty lives. It leaves us at the mercy of our own bad habits.

We really are our own worst enemies. The longer we stay on the path of default, the harder it is to realize that we're missing the life God intended us to live. The longer we put off taking responsibility for our own choices, the harder it is to accept the fact that we are where we are today because of the choices we didn't make.

The courage to explore new options and make new choices is a theme that runs through the entire Bible. The Bible teaches us to embrace the process of change. The teachings of Christ help us understand that adversity makes us stronger.

What if your dream doesn't go the way you planned? What if you have a vision from God? What if you make plans? What if you bring your vision and plans into balance by putting God in the hub of your life? What if you set the wheels in motion… and your dream comes crashing down?

The most exciting day in your life is the day you realize you can do something new. When God interrupts your plan, it's because he wants to show you a bigger plan. If you've given up on your dream, ask God to give you a bigger dream than the one you lost.

And give thanks for the opportunity to keep dreaming.

One Last Riddle

When Sam read the second chapter of Peter's first letter, he realized that John's strange message was "coded" after all:

"You are coming to Christ, who is the living cornerstone of God's temple. He was rejected by people, but he was chosen by God for great honor.

"And you are living stones that God is building into his spiritual temple. What's more, you are his holy priests. Through the mediation of Jesus Christ, you offer spiritual sacrifices that please God. As the Scriptures say,

'I am placing a cornerstone in Jerusalem, chosen for great honor, and anyone who trusts in him will never be disgraced.'

"Yes, you who trust him recognize the honor God has given him. But for those who reject him,

'The stone that the builders rejected has now become the cornerstone.'

"And,

'He is the stone that makes people stumble, the rock that makes them fall.'

"They stumble because they do not obey God's word, and so they meet the fate that was planned for them."

"But you are not like that, for you are a chosen people. You are royal priests, a holy nation, God's very own possession. As a result, you can show others the goodness of God, for he called you out of the darkness into his wonderful light" (1 Peter 2:4-9).

Can you see what Sam saw when he read 1 Peter 2? Let's take a closer look at John's "coded" message:

$$==\!/\!\sim\!o\!\sim\!o\!\sim\!1\!\sim\!Pe\!\sim\!2\!\sim\!o\!\sim\!o\!\sim\!/\!==$$

Do you see the path on either side of the stream? Do you see the banks of the stream? I'm sure you see the four stones and the surging water all around them.

Can you see the stumbling stone? It's the one we read about in 1 Peter 2: The same stone that provides sure footing to help us reach the other side is "the stone that makes people stumble."

If you trust him, you will never be disgraced. If you reject him, he is the rock that will make you fall. It all depends on the choice you make.

At the end of *The Four Stones*, Sam is blind no more. He has discovered his true identity as a "living stone." He is ready to accomplish his goal of showing others how to find their path of purpose and walk in God's wonderful light.

Romans 8:19 says, "For all creation is waiting eagerly for that future day when God will reveal who his children really are." The whole universe is watching, listening, and waiting—waiting to see which path you choose.

Eternity doesn't start when you die. You're already living in Eternity right here, right now. The path on the other side of your obstacle is the kingdom of God. You enter the kingdom here, on earth, when you get on the path of God's purpose for your life.

When your life on earth is over, it will be too late to make a deal with God. Even though you're one of the greatest writers that ever lived, as Charles Dickens was; even though you're the richest man in the world, as Howard Hughes was; even though you're a celebrated Holocaust survivor, as Primo Levi was—this world is your only opportunity to make a choice.

Even though you tell bedtime Bible stories to your children and teach them to be like Christ, you still have to take the last step. Live life by design: Invite Jesus Christ to be your Lord and Savior today. He will strengthen you, give your life new meaning, and help you find your path of purpose.

The last page in this book is reserved for you. It's your reservation for a life of joy, peace, and overflowing hope. It starts when you discover God's plan for your life.

If you're not sure what to write, be still.

Find a peaceful place: a place where you can pray, meditate on the Scriptures you've read in this book, give thanks for God's blessings in your life, and hear his answer.

Ask God to make you a new person by changing the way you think. Then you will know his good and pleasing and perfect will for your life.

"I pray that God, the source of hope, will fill you completely with joy and peace because you trust in him. Then you will overflow with confident hope through the power of the Holy Spirit."

Romans 15:13

Personal Vision Statement

"Your word is a lamp to guide my feet
and a light for my path."
Psalm 119:105

Write down your personal vision statement here.